Praises for *Biblical Counseling*

Based on Dr. Clark's seminary class, "Counseling in the Local Church," we are all now the recipients of this needed and timely book. His reverence for Scripture, scholarship, and pastoral experience help us to navigate the building of biblical counseling ministry in its logical home, the local church.

Barb Bridges, *former director and counselor at Westside Family Church, Lenexa, Kansas*

Like many instances in the Scripture, the man is the message. *Biblical Counseling: A Guide for the Church and Community* is the product of years of ministry and teaching experience. The fruit of his ministry has shown that being available to engage those facing difficulties of life will bring life-giving hope and guidance found in the Scriptures. Dr. Clark has come to meet you, the reader, in this book. You may now be where he was 20 or 30 years ago in ministry: get ready to grow quickly. It has been said that there are two ways to gain ministry wisdom. The first way is to use trial and error with people's lives. The second is to listen to someone wise and experienced who is ready to keep you from his mistakes and to point you toward faithfulness. The latter is obviously the recommended path and the benefit of this book for you and your church. I would invite all who labor hard in ministry to find rest in this refreshing work from a gentle and humble servant of the Lord.

Joshua Clutterham, *Professor of Bible and Biblical Counseling, Brookes Bible College, St. Louis, Missouri*

Dr. Clark joins Drs. Jeremy Lelek's and Heath Lambert's recent offerings in providing the biblical counseling world with some fresh insights while preserving the historic core of the discipline. A refreshing dimension to this work is the demonstration that biblical counseling is not limited to the clinical pastoral office. He shows us how the practice is woven into the fabric of the local church and from the church into the community. Anyone can access the wisdom he offers as he illustrates the correct and practical application of the Word of God to the angst we experience living in this fallen world.

Howard Eyrich, Th.M., D.Min., Retired Pastor of Counseling Director of the Doctor of Ministry Program, Birmingham Theological Seminary; Counselor-at-Large, The Owen Center

---

Truly, a pastor can be overwhelmed by the need in the church for someone to come alongside, and help to guide, comfort, and care for the needs in his congregation. But not all counseling is biblical. Dr. Clark has written this book to encourage those willing to assist by laying a solid biblical foundation for counseling. By presenting the need, the tools, and the calling of this ministry, Dr. Clark walks through a biblical approach to accomplishing the goal of personal restoration with God and His purposes. Our church has benefited from Dr. Clark and the counseling department of Calvary University. We have a graduate who has established a biblical counseling center to serve our congregation and community. As the pastor, I know firsthand that this works and recommend this book to anyone desiring to counsel in the local church.

Darrell Godfrey, former Senior Pastor, Shawnee Bible Church, Shawnee, Kansas

Dr. James Clark draws on his years of experience as a counselor, chaplain, pastor, and Christian university president and professor to equip the body of Christ to meet the needs of a hurting world by providing the practical "how to" of counseling. This book is needed and will change lives!

Vicky Hartzler, *Member of Congress of the United States, House of Representatives, Washington, D.C.*

Finally, a book has been written on biblical counseling that is drawn from a commitment to the sufficiency of the Holy Scriptures and truly honors Christ as our "all in all." Dr. Clark's book is one that all believers can understand, and it gives clear direction on how the church can counsel and serve one another to the glory of God. This is what God intended the church to do!

Charles Hornick, *Academic Dean and Instructor at Frontier School of the Bible*

James Clark writes from experience—vast experience. Remember the old commercial, "When E.F. Hutton talks, people listen"? When James Clark talks about counseling, we should listen. *Biblical Counseling: A Guide for the Church and Community* is our opportunity to listen, learn, and employ.

Dr. Woodrow Kroll, *Creator, The HELIOS Projects*

Dr. James Clark has written this book to motivate and instruct local churches to equip believers to be all they can be in ministering to one another. This is not a new approach or system or program. Rather, it is a challenge for God's people to understand their purpose and function in the local church to be God's instruments for healing broken people. What a high and noble calling! I encourage every pastor and church member to read this book.

Dr. Les Lofquist, *Assistant Professor of Practical Theology, Shepherds Theological Seminary, former IFCA International Executive Director*

Every church is (or should be) a counseling center. Every pastor is (or should be, by his calling) a counselor. As someone who has invested over 30 years building and directing biblical counseling centers, I am happy to endorse this helpful book by Dr. Clark. It provides not only a Scriptural basis for biblical counseling within the local church, but also very practical advice on how to patiently go about establishing such a thing. This book is a concise reference manual for anyone interested in being a part of a biblically-based counseling ministry.

Dr. Lou Priolo, Author, President of Competent to Counsel International

At a time when our world feels uncertain and mental and emotional suffering is widespread, the Word of God is more essential than ever to give guidance. Dr. Clark brings years of experience to this book. He shares powerful and practical illustrations, and also technical insights, but above all, he demonstrates through careful exegetical study and Bible exposition how the Word of God is effective in helping people in the twenty-first century. In Brazil, there is not an abundance of biblical material. As a pastor and counselor, I welcome this book to assist me in effectively helping those who are struggling and in need of guidance.

Leandro Terrataca, Msc. PhD, President of ABECAR Bible College and Theological Seminary, São Paulo, Brazil

BIBLICAL
COUNSELING
A Guide for the Church and Community

Dr. James Clark

LARKSPUR, COLORADO

Grace Acres Press
PO Box 22
Larkspur, CO 80118
www.GraceAcresPress.com

Grace Acres Press also publishes books in a variety of electronic formats. Some content that appears in print may not be available in electronic books.

Print ISBN: 978-1-60265-066-4
E-book ISBN: 978-1-60265-067-1

Library of Congress Control Number: 2019955345

Printed in United States of America
25 24 23 22 21 20   01 02 03 04 05 06 07 08

Acknowledgments

I have a great appreciation for those who served as readers and their excellent feedback as to the content of this book from their fields of expertise: Mrs. Patricia Miller, the former department chair of the biblical counseling program at Calvary University; and Dr. Thomas Baurain, Dean of the Seminary, Professor of Bible and Theology at Calvary University. The proofreaders who toiled over each chapter were Dr. Terri Stricker, former Professor of English at Calvary University; and Dr. Stacy Goddard, our daughter, who is an assistant professor in the Department of Kinesiology, Missouri State University.

My gratitude to my wife, DeLoris, who assisted and encouraged me throughout the writing of this book and believes in its message for the local church and community.

CONTENTS

PART III
Protecting the Church

Closing Thoughts

FOREWORD

This book represents the distilled results of many years of ministry: Youth for Christ, a couple decades of pastoral ministry, and twenty-three years of academic ministry. Dr. James Clark joined the faculty of Calvary Bible College in Kansas City, Missouri (now Calvary University), specifically to begin a program of biblical counseling: first for an undergraduate degree, then a master's degree. In the process he rose to the rank of full professor, then academic dean, and finally became the first alumnus of the school to be installed as president of his alma mater. But he never forgot where the action really takes place.

James Clark has written a book displaying his heart for local church ministry. None of what you will read is theory: it is his life. He has been there, done that, so to speak. Local church ministry requires biblical counseling because local churches are to make disciples, not entertain people. For those who share Clark's concern for local churches that are effective in ministry to their people, this book shows the way. Biblical counseling in the context of the local church setting is nothing less than discipleship in action.

What you will read is not how to start another program. This is not a program, it is the development of a culture of concern for others in the local church. In today's climate, far too many churches are distracted with fads or new "'how to do it'" ideas.

It is time to return to the basics. Dr. Clark lays it out clearly and completely. As a colleague and friend of Jim, it is my privilege to recommend this book to you.

Dr. Thomas S. Baurain
Professor of Bible and Theology
Dean of the Seminary
Calvary University

PREFACE

WHY THIS BOOK?

During my years of serving the Lord as a pastor, many counseling opportunities opened to me, and I realized early in my career the need for further training in knowing how to help people with their problems.

I began my ministry serving as a Youth for Christ director. I found myself spending a great deal of time counseling youth who were dealing with various problems. Many teenagers struggled with family issues, relationships, addictions, human growth and development, and social identity problems—to name just a few. During this time, I was engaged in the lives of young people, spending one-on-one time with them, listening and seeking ways to help them connect their faith, or lack of it, to life issues.

Much of my time was spent helping young people sort through problems at home, such as dealing with divorced parents and living with a single parent. I recall my teenage daughter recounting an experience she had while taking a sociology class at school. The class had broken into small groups to discuss family matters and the difficulties each of them faced at home. One by one, students shared the insecurity of a home life where fighting was common; where they were living with the fear of their parents either separating or going through a divorce; or where they were living with a single parent. My daughter had been quietly listening to the members of her group when her classmates asked her to tell what her home life was like. Her response was very different from the other students': She communicated that her parents loved each other, didn't fight, and there was a loving and stable home environment. Our daughter was disturbed by the group's response because they simply didn't believe she lived in a home like the one she was describing. The group thought she was painting a picture of an ideal home that did not really exist. Sadly, this example shows the state of the family in our society today, with many homes being fragmented and dysfunctional.

Following youth ministry, I became an associate pastor working with the entire family in our church rather than just the youth. While serving in this capacity, I became a chaplain for a local community college and vocational-tech institution. Counseling once again surfaced as an important element of my ministry. For example, one day a couple approached me on campus seeking my counsel about abortion. They were not married, but she was pregnant, and they were considering an abortion. I shared my faith and the position I held related to abortion and informed them of other options they might consider. I prayed with them and felt good about our time together. About a month later I saw them on campus and inquired how they were doing and if they had made a decision about the baby. To my surprise, they told me they were fine and had decided to have the abortion. In reviewing my counsel to them, I realized I had simply communicated what I would do in that situation and what my position was related to abortion, rather than using proper counseling skills that would have led them to fully contemplate their decision and the effect it would have on the rest of their lives, as well as the life of their unborn child. Using a proper counseling approach might not have changed the decision they made to abort their baby, but it clarified to me that I needed to learn better counseling approaches to help lead people to make better, God-honoring choices in their lives.

As the years progressed, I became a lead pastor and once again the Lord provided me the opportunity to do chaplaincy work at the Minnesota State Penitentiary. One of the inmates shared with me that his wife was divorcing him, and his nine-year-old son was having open-heart surgery. His dilemma was that he felt like everything was out of his control. He couldn't talk with his wife and he couldn't be with his son for the surgery. He was frustrated and angry about the situation in which he was living. At the time, I questioned what counsel I could even give him. Here was a man whose world was spinning out of control, and he was looking to my counsel to help him through his anger, resentment, and hopelessness. This is just one example of many inmates who have traumatic life stories and need solid biblical counseling to help them through their difficult situations.

In the next church, I served as lead pastor and also acted as a chaplain for the city's fire and police departments. My first emergency call for the fire department was a home fire; my responsibilities as the chaplain were to keep the family members away from the house and console them as the firefighters tried to put out the fire. At one point I watched with fright as the owner of the house tried to rush back into the house, with a firefighter running up behind him and pulling him away from the burning home. I asked the man why he had tried to get back in the house and, holding his chest, he informed me he had heart problems and was trying to get to the bathroom to retrieve his heart medicine. I realized counseling would have to include more than just talking about problems: at times, action would be necessary to help people in need. For this family, it included getting medical attention, finding temporary housing, dealing with insurance, and helping them cope with the loss of their home and other possessions, as well as helping them with other areas of concern they were presently facing. When I met with them after the night of the fire, they expressed their gratitude that I had been at the scene and offered support and comfort. I was then able to counsel them in dealing with their loss and sharing the hope they could experience by faith in Christ no matter what situation they found themselves facing.

Working as a chaplain for the police department put me in many difficult situations. For example, on one occasion I accompanied a police officer to a home to notify a young lady that her husband had been killed in an accident. As one would expect, people in these types of circumstances are dealing with emotional trauma which leads to the outpouring of other emotions such as denial and anger. I found that in all cases, people were looking to me for answers and solutions to their pain and to help them to make sense of their experiences.

Over my years in ministry, I read many books by known Christian authors in the field of counseling. My experiences challenged me to become knowledgeable and competent as a counselor. I concluded that the people I served trusted me and deserved the best from me. However, it is a daunting task to counsel people through any problem. There are many individuals going through trauma and other serious personal problems with nowhere to turn and desperately seeking someone who can provide guidance and instill needed hope. I also found it encouraging that no one turned me down when I suggested I could pray and read Scripture with them. In their time of need, they were open to the gospel. Even if it was a small window of time, the opportunity was there to counsel them from a biblical worldview.

Over the years of my counseling ministry, I recorded the various problems that people who came to me for counseling were dealing with. The list included addictions (drug, alcohol, and pornography); family difficulties (premarital, separation, divorce, blended family problems, single parenting, incest, sexual abuse, teenage pregnancies, rape, and runaway teens); death-related issues (loss of a loved one from natural causes, accident, murder, suicide, and infant deaths); and emotional or mental problems (manic-depression, eating disorders, phobias, panic attacks, anger, road rage, schizophrenia, sexual deviations, prostitution, and sexually transmitted diseases). Other areas of concern raised by people who sought my counsel included financial problems, midlife crises, legal conflicts, mental disorders … and the list goes on. Unfortunately, this list is not unique. These and many other topics are the norm with people in our churches today.

Through my experiences as a youth pastor, a lead pastor, and then as the person running a biblical counseling center, I have witnessed the need for strong biblical counseling in our churches. Whether used formally or in informal training by pastors and church staff or by people in the pew who want to make a difference in the lives of God's people, I believe this book will help guide anyone who has a heart to counsel others from a biblical worldview.

Counseling: Meeting Needs Through Opportunities

Counseling is ministry. You need to have a compassionate heart supported by and balanced with knowledge of the Word of God that addresses solutions appropriate and relevant for people's souls. The counselor is not someone in an ivory tower, high and mighty, straightening people out with rules and laws. Counseling is hard work; it involves both suffering with people and rejoicing with them. It is exhausting and at times disappointing as well as rewarding. A pastor once told me that ministry should have enough successes to keep one going and enough failures to keep one humble. The counselor must recognize that a spiritual battle is always part of one's counseling ministry.

Never forget, you too are a sinner saved by grace! Leave your piety outside the counseling office, strip off the veneer of righteous indignation, and remember that you are a servant, a slave of the Lord Jesus Christ. You are bringing the cup of water, food, clothing, and visiting the homeless, those in prison, all in the name of Jesus. Your heart is going to ache, the enemy may attack you, and you'll want to give up.

Think twice before you eagerly say, "'I want to be a counselor!'" Counseling consists of dealing with people who are at times very fragile, vulnerable, beaten, and defeated due to sin, either in their lives or from those who have sinned against them. Their troubles may also come from events and circumstances out of their control, such as physical ailments, or disaster from the elements (tornadoes, floods, fires, hurricanes, etc.). As you consider counseling to help people in the church, you will need divine wisdom, strong faith, and a confidence that God is able to transform a life no matter what the issue. Paul challenged young Timothy in 1 Timothy 1:5, But the goal of our instruction is love from a pure conscience and a sincere faith. You therefore, my son, be strong in the grace that is in Christ Jesus.

Over time, I began to formulate a ministry of biblical counseling based on God's Word by utilizing the members of the church (through training and encouragement) to be the body of Christ in ministering one to another. I've also had the privilege to teach a seminary course at Calvary Theological Seminary on the topic "Counseling in the Local Church." This is my conviction and heartbeat for the church. Because of teaching this class, I have seen students go forth and serve in the church as pastors and counselors, as well as chaplains and in other counseling-related positions.

I humbly admit this book will not be a proven, never-fail system claiming, "'Do this and you'll become successful!'" However, the thoughts, ideas, and suggestions in this book will certainly answer a lot of questions you might have about becoming and being an effective counselor.

Having the Right Spirit in Ministry

When I was in the church ministry, I visited a church member who owned a small business in the downtown area. One day I told him that he had a reputation of giving help (money, clothing, etc.) to panhandlers. I advised him that the panhandlers passed on the information about his generosity to others, and that they were taking advantage of him. I asked him why he continued to give to people who were taking advantage of him. He acknowledged that he was aware that some people were just looking for a handout, but then he took me to a back room of his business and pulled out a cigar box that had letters in it. He told me that over the years he had received these letters from a few people who had taken the time to testify to their appreciation for his kindness to them during a time of need when they had nowhere to turn. Some had changed for the good and were most grateful. With tears in his eyes, he looked at me and said, "These letters motivate me to keep giving! From many, a few make proper changes which make all the difference." I left him that day feeling humbled. My visit with him that day started with a spirit of judgment that he needed to stop giving help to streetwalkers, drunks, and down-and-outers. I left with a heart acknowledging that he was a man willing to be taken advantage of to reach a few! Counseling is this way. You give and give in hopes that it will make a difference in the lives of a few.

PART I

The Case for Biblical Counseling

1

The Invasion of a Secular Worldview

"No deity will save us; we must save ourselves, reason and intelligence are the most effective instruments that humankind possesses." Humanist Manifesto II (Preface, 1973)

Since you died with Christ to the basic principles of this world, why, as though you still belonged to it, do you submit to its rules? Colossians 2:20

In the 1960s, as a young man starting in ministry, I was ready to change the world for Christ. Over the years, opportunities have opened for me in youth, church, and parachurch ministries. During these years, the Vietnam War had a philosophical influence on college campuses, where many of the youth rebelled against authority. In fact, the rebellious mindset challenged government, law enforcement, and even the authority of the church.

Our country had accepted Darwin's theory of evolution as well as the development of Freud's psychoanalysis. Sigmund Freud, a Jewish atheist, pointed his finger at the teachings of the Roman Catholic Church and insisted that the doctrine produced false guilt in people's minds. Indeed, he considered those who believed the teachings of the Roman Catholic Church to have a form of mental illness. In addition, secular culture rejected Christianity and denounced the Bible as not being the embodiment of truth and authority (Wright, Jr., 1994, pp. 22, 70, 79).

As a young pastor, chaplain, and counselor, I sought to convince people that the Bible was what they needed. Sadly, many students rejected the message and didn't want to accept the Bible's authority. They preferred to accept various other beliefs, including biological and theistic evolution, naturalism, Eastern philosophies, empiricism, and psychology. Moreover, these diverse influences produced a corrupted marriage in which the church integrated biblical truth with secular thought, embracing social science as creditable and relevant. One must define biblical counseling from a secular or integration point of view. Tautges, in *Counseling One Another* (2015, pp. 21–22) clearly defines biblical counseling as

> an intensely focused and personal aspect of the discipleship process, whereby believers come alongside one another for three main purposes: first, to help the other person to consistently apply Scriptural theology to his or her life in order to experience victory over sin through obedience to Christ; second, by warning their spiritual friend, in love, of the consequences of sinful actions; and third, by leading that brother or sister to make consistent progress in the ongoing process of biblical change in order that he or she, too, may become a spiritually reproductive disciple-maker. Biblical counseling is helping one another, within the body of Christ, to grow to maturity in Him.

For a list of other biblical counseling definitions, see Appendix A.

During my early years as a pastor, I listened to modern-day experts and read their views on theology and counseling. I realized they didn't consider the Bible sufficient or relevant to meet the needs of modern man. In fact, the so-called experts inferred that a pastor wasn't qualified to help people who had deep problematic issues in life, nor was the Bible able to address such needs. In touring the Focus on the Family campus built by James Dobson, I found it interesting that the phone calls from the public who were needing help from someone in their area were referred only to licensed counselors, or to pastors who were on their list as licensed counselors.

Scripture Only? Really?

After preaching in a church one Sunday morning, I was approached by an alumna of Calvary Bible College. Part of my sermon had been about biblical counseling, which I had been teaching. The alumna stated, "I hope you're not one of those Bible-only counselors just dishing out Bible verses as the solution to people's problems." At that moment, I felt severely ostracized for the biblical counseling program that I had established. It was obvious that these church members were disappointed by the direction Calvary was taking in the field of counseling. I swallowed hard and asked if I could read Scripture. Since I was being accused of using Scripture, I might as well stand on God's Word from 2 Peter 1:3–4, which reads:

> *His divine power has given us everything we need for life and godliness through our knowledge of him who called us by his own glory and goodness. Through these he has given us his very great and precious promises so that through them you may participate in the divine nature and escape the corruption in the world caused by evil desires.*

After reading the verses, I asked if they indicated that Scripture is sufficient, or if there was room to add to Scripture because it was inadequate. I'll never forget the response: "Well, if you put it that way, I guess nothing needs to be added." I replied, "I didn't put it that way; this is God's Word speaking, not me."

Even in the Christian community, some have embraced the lie that for the healing of souls, one needs the Bible *plus* something else (psychology, therapy, psychiatry, …). Some would say that the sciences should take precedence over Scripture in the field of mental illnesses—yet these same Christians would vehemently argue with anyone who believes that salvation is by grace *plus* something else, such as good works or church membership. Many in the church today do not see the consistency in the belief that only Scripture is needed for salvation. They mistakenly think that Scripture plus something else is needed to bring about emotional healing, transformation, and sanctification for humankind. Ultimately, the question that must to be answered is this: Is the greatest tool for emotional and spiritual healing the Bible?

The late Dr. Henry Brandt, a trained psychologist who later went into the ministry and is considered by many the "father" of modern-day biblical counseling, coauthored a book titled *The Word for the Wise*, which admonished those who counsel by stating, "Your specialty is a comprehensive knowledge of the Bible and absolute confidence that it is God's sure guide for all people" (Brandt and Skinner, 1995, p. 18). Brandt's words are important because he was a well-respected doctor of psychology who embraced the truth of Scripture above all else.

Early in my ministry, the Baptist Pastor's Choir from Sweden visited our church. My wife and I had the privilege of hosting two of the men in our home for the night. In my conversation with these pastors, I began to talk about books I had found helpful, such as those authored by Francis Schaeffer, John Stott, Charles Ryrie, and others. As I was talking, I could tell they were not familiar with the authors or books I was describing. I asked if they had read books by these contemporary authors and was surprised by their response. One of the pastors stated, "No, the demand for such books is low since they are not translated into the Swedish language." I responded by asking, "What do you read and study?" The answer they gave completely humbled me. Their simple response to my question was, "We read and study the Bible!" I'm a reader and always have been, but I believe many times I read such books to the detriment of reading the Bible. I'm not denying the benefits of reading and studying for academic pursuit. After all, I have been in Christian education for many years. However, a biblical counselor must recognize that the primary tool of ministry is the Word of God! Do not let it take second place to something else.

Culture and the Slippery Slope

Chafer, who wrote *Systematic Theology* (1947), in his day recognized the culture shift in seminaries by stating, "While the seminary student needs as much theology as ever the trend unfortunately is to substitute philosophy, psychology and sociology for theology. This may be somewhat accounted for by the fact that Biblical doctrine is a revelation and the substitutes are within the range of the thinking of the natural man" (p. viii). Chafer's point recognizes that the cultural invasion has influenced the authority of biblical truth.

In *Total Truth* (2004, p. 23), Pearcey wrote: "To say that Christianity is the truth about total reality means that it is a full-orbed worldview. The term means literally a view of the world, a biblically informed perspective on all reality. A worldview is like a mental map that tells us how to navigate the world effectively. It is the imprint of God's objective truth on our inner life."

Pilate said to Jesus, "You are a king, then!" Jesus answered, "You are right in saying I am a king. In fact, for this reason I was born, and for this I came into the world, to testify of the truth. Everyone on the side of truth listens to me." "What is truth?" Pilate asked (John 18:37, 38a). Jesus told his disciples that He was the Way and the Truth and the Life (John 14:6). Keep in mind that this statement is interpreted as meaning that He is the *only* Way, the *only* Truth, and the *only* Life. There is no room here for negotiation. This contrasts with the worldview of the present culture which denies and rejects biblical truth as final authority. Pearcey's hypothesis stated that, "historically, nineteenth-century evangelicals tried to build a moral science that was religiously autonomous — lower-case science based on empirical and rational grounds alone. In doing so, however, they opened the door to full-fledged philosophical naturalism (nature is all that exists). And it was not long before scholars who embraced that philosophy walked right through the door that had been opened for them. They abolished the courses on moral philosophy, replacing them with empirically oriented courses on experimental psychology and sociology that spelled out the full implications of a naturalistic view of human nature. The American university was being secularized" (2004, p. 307). Pearcey continued, "The only worldview that supports the highest aspirations of the human heart is Christianity" (2004, p. 318).

Jesus Christ often classified people into two categories, the wise and the foolish (Matthew 7:24–27, 25:1–13). Those who reject Him as the Truth (only absolute truth) are foolish and those who believe in Him as the Truth are wise (Matthew 25:1–13). This is where the conflict between two worldviews stands or falls. Paul acknowledged the truth of Jesus by stating, *This is good, and pleases God our Savior, who wants all men to be saved and to come to a knowledge of the truth* (1 Timothy 2:3, 4). The apostle John wrote, *But you have an anointing from the Holy One, and all of you know the truth. I do not write to you because you do not know the truth, but because you do know it and because no lie comes from the truth* (1 John 2:20–21).

Both Paul and John agree that God's truth is authoritative and totally reliable.

Movement from Biblical Truth Toward Relativism

In *The Book that Made Your World*, Mangalwadi wrote: "it was the Western Church that gave birth to the university, in its determined and passionate effort to pursue Truth. Following in the train of great universities of Bologna, Paris, Oxford, and Cambridge, America's first institution of higher education, Harvard, was founded upon the motto *Veritas* [truth]. Over the course of the last century, however, the motto has been stripped of all meaning. 'Leading thinkers' within the academy have succeeded in persuading many that 'truth,' as such, is largely a function of social convention" (2011, p. xiv). Mangalwadi went on to quote the late Richard Rorty, arguably one of the most powerfully influential American thinkers of the past forty years: "'The word truth,' he insists, 'has no significant meaning'" (2011, p. xiv).

Once our culture denied authoritative, absolute biblical truth, a substitute system was developed through psychological cognitive development in which all truth is relative. An example of this evolution of moving from biblical truth to relativism is seen in the work of William Perry. Perry comes from a humanistic philosophical worldview. His conclusions have strongly influenced the direction of education, which ultimately has influenced our culture as a whole. Perry, a psychologist and researcher in epistemological development, wrote a book, *Forms of Ethical and Intellectual Development in the College Years* (1970), which was reprinted in 1998. Perry, who was an educational psychologist and former professor of education at the Harvard Graduate School of Education, studied the cognitive development of college-age students during the 1950s and 1960s. He identified nine positions (often simplified to four levels), ranging from dualism to committed relativism, which set the foundation for the development of a cultural shift to today's educational philosophy.

Macie Hall wrote a blog post for *The Innovative Instructor* on "Perry's Scheme—Understanding the Intellectual Development of College-Age Students" (2013). She wrote, "In a nutshell, Perry described the development of Harvard students as progressing from the dualistic belief that things are either true or false, good or evil, through a stage of relativism in which they feel that all beliefs are equally valid, to a stage of commitment to values and beliefs that are recognized to be incomplete and imperfect but are open to correction and further development."

The four main stages identified by Perry are dualism, multiplicity, relativism, and commitment. The system was set up to educate an incoming freshman who enters college to move from the stage of dualism to committed relativism. *Dualism* views knowledge as absolute: things are true or false, right or wrong, good or evil. This is considered a simplistic position regarding reality. Knowledge and belief are based on authoritative sources and are not chosen by the individual. Hall explains that dualism is knowledge received, not questioned; students feel there is a correct answer to be learned.

Multiplicity moves the student a step further. Most knowledge is absolute, but some is not. There will always be gray areas in which there are no simple answers to questions. Hall indicates that there may be more than one solution to a problem, or there may be no solution. The student may conclude that one answer is just as good as another. It is interesting that in the 1960s and 1970s, Perry found a high number of freshmen students entering college beginning in the stage of dualism. In contrast, Hall concluded that freshmen today enter college at the multiplicity level.

Hall identified the next stage, *relativism*, as one in which knowledge is contextual: students evaluate viewpoints based on sources and evidence, and even experts are subject to scrutiny. What Perry and Hall are proposing is for each individual to recognize the need to make choices that, in certain instances, may contradict previous beliefs and conditioning. The student is faced with the dilemma that the gray areas become the rule rather than the exception.

The final stage leads the student to the *committed relativism* level. Perry believes that the intellectual development of committed relativism is where the senior student should be throughout the educational process. This stage is far removed from the simplistic stage of dualism. The senior tolerates other points of view, and comes to accept that all views are fallible, and therefore may change. In contrast to the simple, blind acceptance by faith of the dualist, the individual forms values and beliefs by incorporating elements from many views.

Hall concludes her post by asking, "So why is it important to you as an instructor? Although today dualistic thinking is less prevalent among college-aged students than in Perry's time, most students still come into a college education and perceive the instructor to be the disseminator of truth. As our faculty-centered pedagogies shift to learner-centered approaches, a key to success will be in understanding how students view their acquisition of knowledge."

I concur that students today are expected to explore many views, apply methods of critical thinking, and seek evidence for their choices and decision-making. But to claim that there are no absolutes, no right or wrong and no good and evil, is simply wrong. There are laws — physical, mathematical, spiritual, biological, and cosmological — that are subject to cause and effect and are unchangeable. Not all are relative. One can deny the law of gravity and then jump off a tall building, but no matter how sincere one's belief system is, the test will have consequences proving the contrary.

The church today is facing this cultural battle between truth and relativism. Today, Christians with a biblical worldview must understand and live life consistently. They must examine and assess their thinking when it comes to influences regarding what constitutes truth. Do such influences pass the litmus test of being consistent with biblical truth?

Pearcey wrote, "Genuine worldview is far more than a mental strategy or a new spin on current events. At the core, it is a deepening of our spiritual character and the character of our lives. It begins with the submission of our minds to the Lord of the universe and a willingness to be taught by Him" (2004, p. 24).

Because biblical truth is eternal, it does not evolve over time. Isaiah 40:8 reads, *The grass withers and the flowers fall, but the word of our God stands forever.*

Christians had only God's Word prior to the development of psychology, sociology, and philosophy. Were they limited by not having these modern approaches? Did they find God's Word insufficient to meet their deepest needs? Were they at a loss to find emotional and mental health in their time of despair? How did they cope or survive during difficulties and times of suffering and persecution? Did they find the Bible and its teaching inadequate? Such questions demand consideration and answers as one contemplates the validity of the present worldview. The conclusions drawn will determine the counselor's direction in offering hope and healing for people today.

The behavioral science theories of psychology seem to have a familiar thread running through or associated with all of them. The system philosophically and psychologically held by counseling theorists reveals that there is no standard of authority. For the Christian counselor, authority rests on the Bible as final authority. Secondly, there seems to be a position that denies God (the God of the Bible), and therefore the counseling approach ignores the spiritual aspect of humanity. You must understand that spiritual is often inferred or referred to by the psychological community, but don't be fooled by that. *Spiritual* could refer to mysticism, higher power, New Age, and any number of other things.

Psychology often concludes that humans are basically good, and that their environment influences their behavior. Change the environment and you change the person. It didn't quite work out that way with Adam and Eve, who were in a perfect environment, the Garden of Eden, and yet fell in sin. Environmental change certainly is justified when it comes to at-risk circumstances such as physical and/or sexual abuse, neglect and mistreatment of minors, or any severely unhealthy climate. It must be recognized, however, that the primary place where change must occur is the human heart. The fact is that humans are sinful, which affects their will, thinking, and behavior from a selfish position. Secular theories such as the humanist, behaviorist, psychodynamic, or existentialist approaches make the counselor into a clinical, professional facilitator, analyst, guide, and enabler—which is often insufficient for creating lasting change.

William Glasser, who developed Reality Therapy, has a good system from a secular point of view. Some Christian counselors have used his system in counseling. The premise for this approach is the three R's: face reality, do the right thing, and be responsible. At first glance, this seems to be a proper way to counsel. This system also emphasizes dealing with the present and making the right adjustments in behavior. The outcome will result in feeling good about oneself, which motivates the person to continue making proper adjustments. The flaw in this approach is the unanswered questions as to what reality is, what the right thing is, and what the responsible act or change in behavior is. Glasser's answer to these questions are founded in societal expectations and laws established by local and/or federal courts. Glasser worked with troubled young people, and his system seemed to achieve progress in the lives of youth where law enforcement and other agencies had failed. However, this system also falls short in that societal laws, norms, and standards are always changing. Many laws, including moral laws of the past, have been abandoned and replaced by secular laws that are constantly in flux. Society becomes the final authority as to "correct" behavior, and as changes occur, confusion is created as to what is right and wrong. Historically we see this played out with Israel in Judges 21:25b, which states: *everyone did that which was right in his own eyes* (NKJV). Why? Israel had lost its authority base.

Unlike the secular approach, Scripture has the answer to any crisis or conflict in one's life, and that answer also gives lasting hope. The Biblical approach is clear: there is a right way and a wrong way, right choices and wrong choices, a right direction or wrong direction to follow. The believer looks to the words of 1 John 4:18, 19: *There is no fear in love. But perfect love drives out fear, because fear has to do with punishment. The man who fears is not made perfect in love. We love because he first loved us.*

If it is true that the Bible should be the final authority and it is inerrant, for the Christian counselor, it seems that Scripture should be considered sufficient for all of life's issues. In his dissertation, Denney (2018) quotes Burk, who addressed this position by writing, "A confession of inerrancy requires two concomitant abnegations: (1) a definition of what inerrancy is, and (2) a clear delineation of the hermeneutical and theological implications of such a confession... unless one embraces both the inerrancy and sufficiency of Scripture, then a commitment to inerrancy means nothing."

Sufficiency as it relates to counseling is where the debate lies between biblical counselors and those who hold to a more integrationist position. Denney (2018, p. 13) explained:

> Just as it is essential to define sufficiency, it is also essential to consider its limitations. The scope of Scripture and sufficiency is limited to sanctification: positional, progressive, and ultimate. Scripture is not sufficient to explain how to make every choice we may be confronted with. For example, it will not explain how to replace a tire. Scripture is sufficient to inform us of the impact of every choice we make as it pertains to our sanctification, i.e. what is the God-pleasing choice? Therefore, while Scripture will not tell us how to replace a tire, it does address the issues of sanctification that surround the replacement such as not replacing a tire with a stolen tire, as

that would not be a God-pleasing choice. The commandment of God is, *You shall not steal.* (Ex. 20:15)

In *The Christian's Guide to Psychological Terms* (2004, foreword), Mack summarizes the fact that many Christian pastors and psychologists have ceased to believe that the Bible is sufficient for understanding and solving the problems of life. Unfortunately, many Christians have assumed that the Scriptures are silent on the practical issues on which psychologists/philosophers write and speak. Consequently, they have neglected to do the serious Bible research that is necessary for mining the rich and relevant truths found in Scripture on these practical matters.

The Good and Bad News of Sin

Another characteristic of society and the church is the absence of the word "sin." Both in the secular world and the church, often the emphasis is on self-esteem, a denial of personal responsibility, and victimization rather than biblical truths such as finding your identity in Christ, self-control, and personal responsibility. Sigmund Freud and Carl Rogers both denied the sinfulness of humans.

In *Psychological Seduction*, William Kilpatrick stated, "Christianity doesn't make much sense without sin. If we are not sinners, turned away from God, then there was no reason for God becoming man and no reason for Him to die. Our slavery to sin is the thing that Christ came to free us from. That is the most fundamental Christian belief. We can put the matter more strongly and say that once one grants the notion that people are sinless, then it must mean that Christianity is all wrong" (1983, p. 74). The churches today have ignored the doctrine of sin by emphasizing the message of happiness, self-esteem, meeting personal needs, wealth, health, and success, with very little doctrinal substance and Scriptural exposition.

A book released in the 1990s, *Breaking Free—from the Bondage of Sin* (1994), was discontinued shortly after publication. I called the author, Dr. Henry Brandt, and expressed my surprise and disappointment that it was no longer available, as I was considering using it for a counseling class. Dr Brandt shared that he was also disappointed that it was not available and wasn't sure why. I said, "Dr. Brandt, I think I know why it didn't sell. When looking for books on counseling in a Christian bookstore, this book would be located under the self-help section. It is rare to find a book in this section to have the word 'sin' in the title." He ruefully acknowledged that possibility. It's a sad commentary on the field of counseling that the cultural worldview has invaded the church to this degree, where sin is not acknowledged as a major reason for the problems of today.

The Bible is explicit regarding sin and humanity's problems. In Psalm 51:5, David declares, *Surely I have been a sinner from birth, sinful from the time my mother conceived me.* Additionally, in Psalm 32:5, David prayed, *Then I acknowledged my sin to you and did not cover up my iniquity. I said, I will confess my transgressions to the Lord and you forgave the guilt of my sin.* The angel's message to Joseph in Matthew 1:21 concerned taking Mary to be his wife: *She will give birth to a son, and you are to give him the name Jesus, because he will save his people from their sins.* The Apostle Paul supported the fact that humans are sinful by writing, in Romans 3:23: *for all have sinned and fall short of the glory of God.* To ignore or bypass the fact that sin is the cause of problems is to be a traitor to biblical truth. Kilpatrick wrote, "G. K. Chesterton once observed that the doctrine of fallen man is the only Christian belief for which there is overwhelming empirical evidence" (1983, p. 191).

This is not good news. Sin and evil reside in the heart of each human being. The good news is the gospel of Jesus Christ. All who believe in Jesus Christ for the remission of sin and put their trust in him as Savior and Lord will have eternal life. Brandt and Skinner (1995, p. 18) were accurate when they stated that "Christian counseling is after all the diagnosis of sin."

The fall of man is described in the book of Genesis; we see a pattern of sin, guilt, shame, fear, blame, and separation. Before the fall, man did not experience these issues; he felt no shame (Genesis 2:25). At the fall of man, sin entered the heart of humans, producing shame and guilt (Genesis 3:1–7). By virtue of sin, Adam and Eve covered themselves. We read that when God came to the garden Adam and Eve hid themselves, deliberately separating themselves from God out of fear (Genesis 8–10). After God inquired as to who told Adam he was naked, and if he had eaten of the fruit from the tree, Adam blamed the woman and the woman turned and blamed the serpent (Genesis 11, 12). The consequences of sin are expressed in the way humans think, and are characterized as feeling self-condemning, experiencing bitterness, depression, defeatism, anger, destructive behavior and lifestyle, and so on (Galatians 5:19–22). Some may respond with self-exaltation, characterized by perfectionism, love of self, being driven to excel at all costs, being divisive and judgmental, having a critical spirit, desiring to seek personal recognition, and the like (2 Timothy 3:1–4). The only cure for such thinking and responses is the gospel of Jesus Christ, which brings freedom from the bondage of sin by His grace and forgiveness. Due to this liberation from sin, the believer responds with thanksgiving and gratitude for all God has done by His marvelous grace on the believer's behalf. As 1 Thessalonians 5:18 admonishes, *in everything give thanks; for this is God's will for you in Christ Jesus.*

The Apostle Paul warned the Colossian church about a culture that is deceptive, destructive, and persuasive. The warning was to watch out and not to be caught in a web of godless ideology. Paul admonished the church, *See to it that no one takes you captive through hollow and deceptive philosophy, which depends on human tradition and the basic principles of this world rather than on Christ* (Colossians 2:8).

John recognized the threat of a false worldview and passionately challenged the believers in 1 John 4:4–6: *You, dear children, are from God and have overcome them, because the one who is in you is greater than the one who is in the world. They are from the world and therefore speak from the viewpoint of the world, and the world listens to them. We are from God, and whoever knows God listens to us; but whoever is not from God does not listen to us. This is how we recognize the Spirit of truth and the spirit of falsehood.*

I realize I have shared my conviction about counseling and the social sciences. I find Scripture to be very persuasive in warning the church about humanity's ideologies. However, a Christian counselor may find merit in studying certain disciplines in psychology and psychiatry, such as physiological conditions affecting emotions and behavior, military studies regarding the effects of traumatic battlefield experiences, human growth and development, police criminology, and so on. In *Psychological Seduction* (1983, p. 74), Kilpatrick wrote, "Psychology as a science has a legitimate part to play in our society. It is another matter when it wants to play every part and direct the drama as well." I find that the issue is not what is observed in studies of human behavior; rather, the issue is the psychologist's interpretation of such studies. Kilpatrick concludes, "The issue must be viewed according to one's interpretation of the data. Will the interpretation come from a biblical worldview or from a philosophy that rejects such a worldview?" (1983, p. 191).

Jones, in *The Counsel of Heaven on Earth*, agrees with this argument, writing:

> All secular counseling theories have one principle in common: the individual and the society are at the center of all change; they are the source of both the problems and

the potential solutions in life. These theories focus on the horizontal dimension of relationships, but they ignore the divine or vertical dimension. They are built on a philosophy of naturalism, which acknowledges the existence only of material, measurable, observable, natural elements or forces in the world, to the exclusion, by definition, of the supernatural or spiritual (2006, p. 150).

David Powlison made the argument for the position of biblical counseling in the book *Psychology and Christianity*:

Sin has typical effects on theorizing, and the secular psychologies manifest a profound paradigmatic commonality. All agree that human beings are autonomous rather than responsible to an objective God who acts and speaks. All agree that the problem with people is anything but sin, and problems can be explained in purely psychological, psychosocial, or psychosocial somatic terms. All agree in positing some sort of determining factor to replace choice either for or against God as the central, specific, and pervasive issue of human existence. All agree that both answers and power to change reside either in the individual, in human relationships, or in medical chemistry. All agree that anything but Jesus Christ and the ministry of the Word will be the answer to sin and misery, that is, to our dysfunctions, dysphoria, and syndromes. All busy themselves trying to prove that anything but Christianity's view of things is true (in Johnson & Jones, 2000, pp. 208–209).

I conclude that the study of the soul belongs to the biblical doctrine of anthropology. Genesis 1:27 reveals God's creative purpose for humanity: *So, God created man in his own image, in the image of God he created him; male and female he created them.* This is where we must start in understanding humans as created beings, fallen in sin, yet with the opportunity to respond to the grace of

God for the redemption of their souls. Denying this foundational truth leaves humans in constant search like the blind man in a dark room looking for a black cat that isn't there. The believer's hope, however, is expressed in Romans 6:17–18: *But thanks be to God that, though you used to be slaves to sin, you wholeheartedly obeyed the form of teaching to which you were entrusted. You have been set free from sin and have become slaves to righteousness.*

The counselor must consider making a conscious choice between two philosophies, the secular worldview or the biblical worldview. A frightening statement I heard from Dr. Norm Geisler was that 92% of Christian America does not have a biblical worldview. This presents a challenge to the biblical counselor who counsels those in the Christian community. The Apostle Paul stated it well: *Do your best to present yourself to God as one approved, a workman who does not need to be ashamed and who correctly handles the word of truth* (2 Timothy 2:15).

Looking Ahead

The next chapter describes the uniqueness of the local church. The church is an organism, not an organization. The church is a collective body of believers gathered to minister to one another, to serve one another, and to edify one another. In the context of personal relationships where Christ is the Head of the church, an environment is established for counseling one another.

2

The Uniqueness of the Local Church in Counseling

And He put all things in subjection under His feet and gave Him as head over all things to the church, which is His body, the fullness of Him who fills all in all. (Ephesians 1:22, 23, NASB)

———————— ⌣ ————————

This verse acknowledges that Christ is the head of the church. He builds His church, which is His priority, and second to none as a model and example before the world.

A seminary student in my biblical counseling class was working at a hospital in the mental health unit. After class, he came to me and shared his frustration with the hospital system. His supervisor had put him on warning that he was to stop giving patients Christian literature and sharing Christian values in small-group sessions. He indicated that he had handed out devotional material at the request of a patient and shared his personal faith after a patient indicated a need for having faith. The supervisor felt that Christianity was a crutch and informed the student that Christianity was not the purpose of the mental health department. The student felt like his hands were tied, and he recognized that much of what they were doing there was just keeping the patients medicated.

This story is an example of two contrasting philosophies about helping people. In examining such approaches, the church of Jesus Christ is truly unique, vastly different from the model of the world. God is the healer of the heart and soul of all humanity. The words of the prophet Jeremiah in chapter 17:9, 10 describe this clearly: *The heart is deceitful above all things and beyond cure. Who can understand it? I, the Lord, search the heart and examine the mind, to reward a man according to his conduct, according to what his deeds deserve.*

The question of who can understand the heart of man is clearly answered here: God alone is the only one who searches the heart, and tests the mind, and the only one who accurately judges each person according to that person's ways and deeds. The prophet Isaiah also supports this conclusion, stating in 48:17 (NASB): *This is what the Lord says—your Redeemer, the Holy One of Israel: I am the Lord your God, who teaches you what is best for you, who directs you in the way you should go.* Once again, the argument is that God is the healer and provides the way that humanity should go.

Community of Believers

In the New Testament, God's model for this age is found in the church of Jesus Christ. The church is not an organization but rather an organism, a collective body of believers who are gathered together to minister to one another. This body of believers is the church. The Greek term, *ekklesia*, which means a called-out assembly, became the word for believers gathering together into a new community. In the *Expository Dictionary of Bible Words*, Richards wrote, "This community is committed to Jesus and to the radical lifestyle expressed in God's Word. It is the allegiance of the new community to Jesus that makes its members different from those 'outside'" (1985, p. 164).

Dr. Richards's description of the church defines it as a loving community designed to assist one another. This community is an environment with a model of mentoring, discipling, and equipping each member to become healthy and strong in the Lord spiritually. This model recognizes the spiritual component as central in all problems. By emphasizing the spiritual aspect in an individual, rather than ignoring, denying, or evading the spiritual issue, the individual becomes encouraged and hopeful that healing is possible through the Word of God and connection with the community of God's people, the church.

Think back to the student who worked at the hospital in the mental health unit. All patients desperately needed care. They were institutionalized and medicated. They could not look to each other for healthy support and encouragement due to the severity of their own conditions. The staff was limited by having to avoid the spiritual component that would lead to healing. Everyone had problems, no one had the total solution to their problems, and they did not have a healthy environment to facilitate healing. If one ignores the spiritual aspect of humanity, one will always come up short in ministering to the total person. The biblical philosophy recognizes that God has created humans with five distinct characteristics: physical, emotional, social, mental, and spiritual. All five areas must be considered to appropriately help people. A counselor should explore all areas of an individual to explain how that person's problem has influenced the individual. Throughout this process, a counselor should consider the community of believers who can come alongside and assist an individual toward healing.

A couple came to me for counseling. She was a petite, well-dressed, middle-aged woman. Her husband was overweight, dressed sloppily, and looked like he had not combed his hair. His speech was rather harsh and loud. As we discussed the reason they were seeking counseling, the wife spoke first. With tears in her eyes and mascara beginning to run down her cheeks, she described what she felt was the problem. She indicated that they had terrible communication between them. "He doesn't connect with me, nor does he seem to care. His life revolves around his job as a high school football coach. He puts in many hours at the school and there doesn't seem to be anything that we have in common." I asked the husband how he saw their problem. He acknowledged that his wife was right about their communication issues and said that he was at a loss as to how to communicate to and with her.

I made a luncheon appointment with him to further discuss how he might communicate with his wife. At the lunch I shared a plan: Take her out to dinner and use that time to inquire about her thoughts regarding five specific areas. Ask her questions in each category, such as **Emotional**—what makes you happy and what makes you sad? **Social**—what social events do you enjoy and what friends do you enjoy being with? **Mental**—What do you do to stimulate your mind? What do you like to read? What worries in life do you think about? When you think of life, what would you like to see changed? Are there things you would like to share with me and discuss in this area? **Physical**—ask questions as to her health; does she worry about any health issues? What does she do to stay healthy in weight control, eating properly, exercise, and sleeping? If she could change anything in her appearance, what would it be? Lastly, ask her about her **Spiritual** life: Where is she on her journey of faith? Is she pleased with her church life? Why or why not? What does she pray about? Is she involved in reading the Bible? Where does she need to grow as a Christian? What hinders her from growing in the Lord? Finally, after discussing these five aspects of her life, ask her how she sees him involved in her life; is he being sensitive and encouraging to her?

When they came for their second session, I began by asking how their week went. The wife started first, and suddenly the tears began to flow again. I thought to myself, "Oh no, he has blown it." She quickly composed herself and said, "These are tears of joy. For the first time in years we had a delightful evening together as we went out to eat. My husband was great. We sat and talked for over an hour. We talked, and he seemed very sincere and interested in me and my life. Dr. Clark, I don't know what you said to him that day the two of you had lunch, but I want to thank you so much." I looked at the husband and he just gave me an approving smile that said, "I did good, didn't I?" This was the breakthrough start for this couple in which their relationship began to grow.

Some years ago, I attended a seminar, titled "Step 2," in which a statement caught my attention: "… the church was here on earth, not to do what other groups can do, but to do what no other group of human beings could possibly do, which is to manifest the life and power of Jesus Christ in fulfillment of the ministry which was given by the Father." This statement underscores the uniqueness and purpose of the local church. God's design and plan is for the church to be the vehicle for bringing about healing and wholeness of the individual. Only the church recognizes the importance of the spiritual component of humanity and considers it a priority. The spiritual influences the other four aspects of life. This provides a proper platform for believers to grow in their faith. The Apostle Peter stated the essence of how believers are to consider one another in 1 Peter 3:8: *Finally, all of you, live in harmony with one another; be sympathetic, love as brothers, be compassionate and humble.*

The church today is often tempted to project success through big budgets, multiple programs, large buildings, state-of-the-art technology, major drama events, concerts, and multiple staff specialists. The concern is motivation, purpose, and outcome. If success is measured by this list, the church has missed the mark. The society of Western culture can say to the church, we can match that. Society can build beautiful buildings, claim large bank accounts, and point to artistic accomplishments; however, if that is what constitutes success, society can always exceed what the church claims in being successful. So, what is the benchmark that makes the church unique?

The Church's Calling

The church represents a group of believers collectively serving one another in community and fellowship, to reveal in the world the glory of God's character, found in His Son, Jesus Christ. The believers of the church are to strive to be Christ-like, serving one another. 1 Peter 2: 9–10 reads, *But you are a chosen race, a royal priesthood, a holy nation, a people for God's own possession. So that you may proclaim the excellency of Him who has called you out of darkness into his marvelous light; for you once were not a people, but now you are the people of God; you had not received mercy, but now you have received mercy.*

The church is a priesthood of believers. In the religion of Judaism, only a select group functioned as priests; in contrast, under the new dispensation of the church in Christ's community, all enter the priesthood to represent and carry the needs of the people before God. What a tremendous privilege believers have to pray, counsel, edify, and encourage one another! Yet church upon church fails to recognize, utilize, and take advantage of this ministry before God.

For the first 300-plus years, the community of believers did not gather in buildings, but in homes. Examples of this arrangement are the church of Philippi, which met in the home of Lydia (Acts 16:13–16), and in Colossae, where the home of Philemon (Philemon 1, 2) was a meeting place. Such meetings were intimate with encouragement, fellowship, and teaching of God's Word.

Acts 2:42–47 describes the nature of the early church as a microcosm. The believers met for teaching, fellowship, and sharing, showing hospitality to one another and worshipping together. The church developed into a reservoir of resources, both physical and spiritual, for meeting the needs of the people. They served and supported one another. They extended the gift of hospitality to each other. The church became the source of a potentially abundant supply of resources to persons in need. This concept of hospitality provided a community or family atmosphere where the home/church was intimate and conducive to fellowship. In this way, the church established service and love to all.

The ministry of hospitality seems to be a neglected vehicle of ministry today. When I served in a local church as an associate pastor, we had a couple who effectively ministered to the hurts and needs of others. They were constantly inviting couples to their home, providing a meal, and then using the time to counsel their guests regarding problems those guests were facing. Many families found hope from this couple who opened their home, hearts, and lives to these families. Marriages were saved; individuals were edified and encouraged because they had found help from a couple who reached out, and loved them, and shared the Word of God with them. They read Scripture together, prayed, and worshipped God. Such ministry cannot be duplicated by the world through sterile, institutional, and impersonal professionalism. Scripture emphasizes the importance of hospitality. For example, Romans 12:13 states that believers should practice hospitality by c*ontributing to the needs of the saints, practicing hospitality.* Other verses, such as *Do not neglect to show hospitality to strangers…* (Hebrews 13:2) and *Be hospitable to one another without complaint* (1 Peter 4:9), command believers to be hospitable. Furthermore, hospitality is a requirement for overseers and elders in the church (1 Timothy 3:2; Titus 1:8). *Hospitality* carries the meaning of hosting and welcoming strangers, taking them in and providing loving care for them. From the word hospitality, we get the words hospice and hospital, which is a place to serve strangers or to show affection (love). Hospitality is how the home cultivates affectionate, deep love for one another. Acts 2:46, 47 describe the early church and hospitality: *Every day they continued to meet together in the temple courts. They broke bread in their homes and ate together with glad and sincere hearts, praising God and enjoying the favor of all the people.*

This context of hospitality provides the platform for counseling and ministering to one another. The local church has the means to facilitate the resources of the members in meeting nearly all the needs of those who are struggling with issues in their lives. As people in the church open their homes for small-group Bible study, counseling in their homes, using their homes to listen and pray with others, ministry happens. The home often breaks down barriers and creates an environment to bridge one with another. This type of hospitality seems to be the common denominator in developing the Christian fellowship of the early church found in Acts 2.

Other illustrations of those who were hospitable include Abigail, who served David and his men (1 Samuel 25); and Martha, who opened her home to Jesus and his disciples (Luke 10:38–42). Paul, Barnabas, Silas, Peter, and others needed hospitality from others during their travels. Such examples do not necessarily include the context of counseling, but they do show the role of serving one another to meet needs.

The Apostle Paul, writing to the believers in the Roman church, showed confidence in the believers by stating: *And concerning you, my brethren, I myself also am convinced that you yourselves are full of goodness, filled with all knowledge and able also to admonish one another* (Romans 15:14, NASB). In *An Expository Dictionary of New Testament Words* (1966, p. 31), Vine explains that the word "admonish" carries the meaning of to warn through instruction. Paul continues this conviction in Colossians 3:16: *Let the word of Christ richly dwell within you, with all wisdom teaching and admonishing one another....*

Paul conveys that "to admonish" is not reserved for the pastors/ overseers of the church; it includes all believers. The significance of this is underscored in the use of the word *laos*, which refers to the people of God or all believers. The local church is a reservoir of gifted believers able to minister to the needs of others. Church leadership should never underestimate this great potential God has provided for the local body of believers.

The following chapters of the book of Acts build on the growth of fellowship of the communities of Christ, and the Epistles reflect the development and growth of churches throughout Asia Minor and the impact upon city after city, country after country, where the fingerprint of the church affected the pagan societies it touched. The church was identified with terms like *family, community, body* (body of Christ), *marriage*, and *fellowship*. Richards wrote: "To live together as Christ's church calls for the development of close personal relationships, for the ministry of members to one another, for the experience of family love, and for maturing in holiness. The believing community is to learn how to relate to Jesus corporately and is to build a lifestyle that reflects corporate as well as individual" (1985, p. 164).

From *Eerdmans' Handbook* (1977, p. 37), we get a sense of the early years of the church:

> The hallmarks of apostolic Christianity were simplicity, community, evangelism and love. It was simple because it had little or no formal organization, maintained no church buildings or membership rolls, taught easy-to-understand doctrines, and followed a plan of financing activities by personal giving. In addition, the Christian emphasis on a community of love sealed by baptism appealed to many people who were otherwise without hope and desperately lonely. Many felt themselves adrift in a world grown too large, and they craved the type of intimate fellowship offered by the Christian congregations.

The Church Ministers by Serving One Another

The Apostle Paul outlines the structure and purpose of the church in Ephesians 4:11–13 (NASB): *And He gave some as apostles, some*

*as prophets, and some as evangelists, and some as pastors and teachers,
for the equipping of the saints for the work of service, to the building up
of the body of Christ; until we all attain to the unity of the faith, and
of the knowledge of the Son of God, to a mature man, to the measure
of the stature which belongs to the fullness of Christ.*

Once again, we see Paul emphasizing that every believer is to
serve the Lord by serving one another. The foundation built
upon by the apostles and prophets and followed by evangelists,
pastors (shepherds), and teachers was intended to equip the
saints for works of service. This is the ministry, with everyone
participating, growing, and serving and building (edifying) one
another. In Ephesians 4: 16, Paul further explains this principle:
*proper working of each individual part, causes the growth of the body
for the building up of itself in love.*

Paul is emphasizing what the student at the beginning of this
chapter longed to do: help people to understand the spiritual
component that would bring about eternal changes in lives of
hurting people. It appears to this writer that the system in which
the student found himself was not an environment conducive to
ministering to the total person; instead, he was mandated to leave
out the spiritual component, with the threat of being terminated
if he continued using faith talk. He found himself in a system
that was far from the reality of a caring community.

Diversity in the Body of Christ

The system of society falls short when the spiritual aspect of
humanity is ignored. Secular society gathers people in groups,
all with similar problems, and allows them to share and vent
their personal experiences in life. I see three problems with this
approach. First, solutions are minimal, as the nature of the group
is merely to listen to, support, and empathize with one another.
Second, the leader of the group simply facilitates the sharing
process by seeking to get people to be vulnerable and express

where they are with their emotions, hurts, and recovery. Third, the group is missing a clear model or picture of what one should look like when fully recovered. The group is not diversified with people who have overcome their problem(s) spiritually, emotionally, mentally, socially, and physically.

When I was a young boy, I began taking piano lessons. A relative of mine asked me what I wanted for Christmas. I informed her that I wanted the recording (long-playing record album) of Van Cliburn playing Rachmaninoff's Concerto No. 3 (performed at Carnegie Hall). Her response was interesting: "But you'll never be as good as Van Cliburn at playing the piano, so why would you want the album?" I've thought about what she said that day and my answer to her could have been, "I probably will never be able to play the piano like Van Cliburn, but why would I want a recording by someone who plays as I do?" My point here is to recognize that Van Cliburn represented what a piano player *should* sound like. I would listen to him (the model player) and enjoy his ability to play the piano correctly.

Likewise, the church of Jesus Christ is comprised of mature role models who can show (demonstrate) the way for others. Those who struggle are not isolated from the body of believers. They are integrated within the group. Through observing and interacting with other believers, they begin to grow and develop in Christlikeness.

In 1 Corinthians 12, Paul wrote about the role of the body of believers and the diversity of the parts as they relate to one another. In verse 11 he wrote, *Now the body is not made up of one part but of many.* Verse 18 continues, *But in fact God has arranged the parts in the body, every one of them, just as he wanted them to be. If they were all one part, where would the body be? As it is, there are many parts, but one body.* Verses 25–27 say *there should be no division in the body, but that its parts should have equal concern for each other. If one part suffers, every part suffers with it; if one part is honored, every part rejoices with it. Now you are the body of Christ, and each one of you is a part of it.*

The Scriptural Mandate for the Church

I'm writing this book to encourage the people of God to support the Scriptural mandate for the church to be the church of Jesus Christ. I am not suggesting a new approach, system, or program. I desire that the church should go about equipping believers to be all they can be in ministering one to another.

The Scriptural foundation is now in place with the purpose and function of the local church as God's design for healing. Its uniqueness is unmatched by any system created by humans alone. Chapter 3 focuses on organizing the local church to be effective in ministering one to another.

PART II

Developing Counseling Training and Structure

3

Developing Church Leadership

Jesus said to Peter, in Matthew 16:18 (NASB), *I will build my Church; and the gates of Hades will not overpower it.* The book of Acts describes the birth and early activities of the church, and the Epistles further explain the developmental growth, organization, and purpose of the church. The Apostle Paul instructed Timothy to multiply the work of the Lord by identifying *reliable men who will also be qualified to teach others* (2 Timothy 2:2). This includes training and teaching others and having them do likewise.

On the subject of seeking qualified leaders, Paul wrote, *And the Lord's servant must not quarrel; instead, he must be kind to everyone, able to teach, not resentful. Those who oppose him he must gently instruct, in the hope that God will grant them repentance leading them to a knowledge of the truth, and that they will come to their senses and escape from the trap of the devil, who has taken them captive to do his will* (2 Timothy 2:24–26). The thread that runs throughout Paul's writings stresses the need to select qualified persons of character who can teach and disciple others with good doctrine and Scriptural conviction.

In *Biblical Leadership*, Gangel wrote:

> Good leaders protect their people more than they protect their buildings, their desks, their papers, their files, their computers, and all other nonhuman resources. No resource in a ministry organization is more important for the fulfillment of objectives than people. If you don't have good people, then it really doesn't matter what else you have. A good computer is not going to solve your problems. Good people may. (2006, p. 37)

The Role of the Pastor

The pastor serves the church in directing the church's ministry. He articulates the vision and mission of the church to the body of believers. His primary focus should be to teach, train, and lead members to Christlike maturity. The pastor must take to heart Paul's admonition (2 Timothy 2:2, 24–26) and Gangel's challenge that the priority of leadership is working with good people. His calling will include protecting the members from false doctrine and seeking unity and harmony within the church. His life models a heart that is gracious and caring, exemplifying love in healing for those who are hurting. He gives biblical counsel by encouraging, edifying, and bringing hope and grace for those in need. He is committed to praying fervently for the flock and to ministering as an example to all through selfless service.

Indeed, the roles of the local church and of the pastor are unique from other organizations and systems of society. In *Brothers, We Are Not Professionals* (2002, p. 1), Piper clarifies this distinction:

> Pastors are being killed by professionalizing the pastoral ministry. The mentality of the professional is not the mentality of the prophet. It is not the mentality of the slave of Christ. Professionalism has nothing to do with the essence and heart of the Christian ministry. The more professional we long to be, the more spiritual death we will leave in our wake. For there is no professional childlikeness (Matt. 18:3); there is no professional tenderness (Eph. 4:32); there is no professional panting after God (Ps. 42:1).

Pastors must view their calling as a unique privilege to serve and minister to their congregation. Such a privilege is reflected by their participation with their people in events such as the birth of their children, marital anniversaries and retirements, special school activities, and other activities in the lives of God's people. The pastor ministers to his people during times of suffering and hardship, transitions of life, sickness, and death. The congregation looks to the pastor for wise, godly counsel regarding life issues such as marital, family, career, financial, emotional, and spiritual experiences in life.

Peter the Apostle clarified the role of the pastor. In 1 Peter 5:2, 3 he wrote, *Be shepherds of God's flock that is under your care, serving as overseers — not because you must, but because you are willing, as God wants you to be; not greedy for money, but eager to serve, not lording it over those entrusted to you, but being examples to the flock.* Notice Peter's emphasis here: The elders are considered shepherds who feed and care for the flock. This is the key assignment given to the elders or shepherds. Historically, the Lord brought judgment upon shepherds of Israel who did not fulfill their calling. An example is Ezekiel 34:2: *Son of man, prophesy against the shepherds of Israel; prophesy and say to them: "this is what the Sovereign Lord says: woe to the shepherds of Israel who only take care of themselves! Should not shepherds take care of the flock?"* The Lord gave a similar statement through Zechariah 11:15–17a: *Then the Lord said to me, Take again the equipment of a foolish shepherd. For I am going to raise up a shepherd over the land who will not care for the lost, or seek the young, or heal the injured, or feed the healthy, but will eat the meat of the choice sheep, tearing off their hoofs. Woe to the worthless shepherd, who deserts the flock!* This is a serious backdrop to Peter's description of the elders/shepherds in 1 Peter. He continues to exhort those in this office by stating that they are to be examples to the flock; they are to lead, teach, train (equip), feed, and care for the flock. He does this by example, through humility (5:1–6), recognizing that he is accountable to the Chief Shepherd. What a great, yet serious, calling for the pastor of a local church!

The amount of counseling done by the pastor varies from pastor to pastor. The size and demographics of the church often affect the pastor's counseling load. I have heard testimonies by pastors who have conducted counseling sessions up to four hours at a time.

Considering all the pastoral responsibilities that the pastor faces, he needs to be reminded that he is not called to be a full-time counselor. Regardless of the size of the church or the needs of the people, the pastor would do well to restrict his counseling time to no more than six to eight hours a week. He must factor in time for counseling preparation, which includes studying, research, and prayer. The pastor must fight the tyranny of the urgent. Many calls appear to be life-threatening emergencies. A primary rule in pastoral counseling is to make sure the counselee is investing as much work, time, and effort as the pastor. Monitoring the counselee's involvement and commitment helps to eliminate the temptation to take advantage of the pastor's time.

In my interviews with pastors, certain attitudes surfaced regarding counseling. Some pastors are uncomfortable doing counseling, thinking that they are incompetent, that they don't have time, or that it is not their priority; they would rather spend their time in sermon preparation or other pastoral duties. Many pastors struggle with keeping a balance in their ministries and personal lives. Eventually, a pastor may become overwhelmed and challenged by trying to fulfill all his responsibilities.

In a survey of 758 Australian pastors, one pastor commented,

> In a regular leadership role in corporate America, you don't have as much dealings with people's emotional stress in their lives. As pastors, when we counsel, we deal with some of the down and dirty stuff in people's lives. And, I don't think you can help but absorb some of that. Other pastors commented that they lacked training. They felt unprepared for conflict resolution, one-on-one counseling, or family counseling. Some pastors had a lack of confidence in their ability to lead others in crisis and decision-making[;] they noted that followers expected guidance from pastors as well as an expanding role of the pastor for pastoral counseling. (Hessel, 2014, p. 170)

The more the pastor is involved in the lives of the people, the more he understands their struggles. Therefore, as he communicates to his congregation through his preaching, teaching, and counseling, he will find that his experiences with people will give confidence and support his theology through practical application regarding life issues. Forsyth (n.d.) said it well, "You must live with people to know their problems and live with God in order to solve them."

Church Leaders Complement the Pastoral Staff

The pastor today is very active in overseeing the church's ministry. Many pastors do not have multiple staff to assist them in meeting all the pastoral demands of the church. The pastor who is honest will come to the realization that the ministry is more demanding than he can accomplish alone. To whom does the pastor turn? The answer is found in the lay leadership represented in the church. Wise is the pastor who invests by pouring his life into the lives of talented people who have great ministry potential. Therefore, the pastor prioritizes the part of his job description that deals with investing in the teaching and training of leaders.

A former church member approached me and said, "Pastor, it's too bad you can't be like a coach and trade your bad players with another church's good ones." I realized he was saying this with tongue in cheek, but as a pastor, I realized there was hidden truth to his statement that I secretly believed. The temptation is to look to "greener pastures" in numbers of people, or finer facilities and programs, and compare another ministry to one's own. The pastor begins to think, "If only our church consisted of influential, wealthy, and gifted people as found in other churches, we, too, would be successful." Such pastors go from church to church in hopes of finding the right combination for success. As the pastor constantly looks elsewhere for the utopian church, eventually he will become disillusioned, discouraged, and leave the ministry.

After listening to the church member, I responded by saying, "Jesus had the opportunity to call men of stature when he chose his disciples." The disciples did not exactly meet the modern-day criteria for leaders! Jesus took His raw material of uneducated, uninfluential, unskilled men and He poured his life into them. He took his team of unknown, common men and He invested his life into them for three years of teaching and divine example. What happened? These men turned the world upside down with a life-changing message for all people!

The leadership team must be a cohesive group with teachable hearts, desirous of serving with willing spirits for ministry. Not all will become teachers or counselors, but they all should understand their place to serve.

Creating a Ministry Mentality

The church leadership must have a conviction and mindset for modeling before the church how they minister to each other. Church board meetings must be restructured to be more than business meetings. Ministry begins here, where people meet and minister one to another through sharing, praying, and growing together in the Lord. The meeting must be used to edify, encourage, and challenge each other in seeking each person's place in ministry. It is a place of accountability as to their role of service. These people must grapple with how God by the Holy Spirit has equipped and gifted them to serve the body of Christ. This takes time, yet it sets the tone for their priority as leaders. The leadership comes to explore what God has for their church through them. Such a process should excite the members to see that they are not just going through the motion as leaders, but rather that they are seeing the significance of their place in the church.

Leaders Set the Pace

Training becomes vital for the leadership. Training should include such areas as theology, counseling, spirituality, church vitality, discipleship, and fellowship issues in carrying out a caring ministry. As leaders begin to implement what they are learning throughout the training sessions, the more they develop a spiritual ministry that matters for them and the church. Through this process, church leaders begin to see God using and working through them to make a difference in the lives of people.

The trained leaders become involved in various areas of ministry, which may include seeking ways to connect with others before and after the worship service by reaching out to those in the congregation. Such leaders would be assigned to welcome visitors and connect them to others in the church. They may be involved in care groups, small group ministries, and other programs that provide participation opportunities for trained leaders.

This spirit of ministry begins to permeate the entire congregation. The servant leaders become motivated to gravitate toward others to minister in a renewed way. They are not driven by a program but by the Holy Spirit.

Developing a Purpose Statement

The leadership communicates the heartbeat and the purpose of the ministry to the congregation. Through prayer and much discussion, the leadership should put in print both a philosophy of ministry and a mission statement that the church will follow. A sample mission statement and philosophy of ministry may state the purpose and philosophy in this way:

Mission Statement

Our purpose, according to God's Word, is to be the people of God who live out the Good News of Jesus Christ. Under the guidance of the Holy Spirit, we desire to lead people into a maturing relationship with Jesus Christ through corporate worship, community outreach, discipleship, and fellowship. Our mission is to enable our people out of love and grace to impact the community and the world.

Philosophy of Ministry

Our philosophy is to utilize all ministries of the church as opportunities for the members to serve where their passion of ministry might be. All ministries should be in a context of openness, spiritual freedom, positive affirmation, and encouragement, with a desire to foster strong personal faith in which God's people, gifted by the Holy Spirit, are being used to their full potential.

Once a church establishes a mission statement and philosophy of ministry, a platform is set for ministering one to another. The community of believers begins ministering in an atmosphere of a loving, caring, fellowship that is committed to building one another up in the faith.

Leaders Lead

The pastors and leaders set the pace in modeling, before the congregation, biblical leadership as God's servants in ministry. Paul wrote to Timothy, *The things which you have heard from me in the presence of many witnesses, entrust these to faithful men who will be able to teach others also* (2 Timothy 2:2). Paul is challenging Timothy to multiply the work of the Lord by identifying reliable persons who can teach and lead others. This includes training others and discipling them so they can teach and train others as well. In the book of Titus, Paul describes the qualifications of elders: *For the overseer must be above reproach as God's steward, not self-willed, not quick-tempered, not addicted to wine, not pugnacious, not fond of sorted gain, but hospitable, loving what is good, sensible, just, devout, self-controlled, holding fast the faithful word which is in accordance with the teaching, so that he will be able both to exhort in sound doctrine and to refute those who contradict.* (Titus 1:7–9, NASB)

Paul continued the list of qualifications for leaders in 1 Timothy 3 as well as in 2 Timothy 2:24–26. It is evident from these passages that Paul is pressing the leadership of the church to lead the way as men of integrity and humility. They are to have a servant's heart, be able to teach with knowledge of the Word of God, be doctrinally sound, mature in the faith, and respected by all. After the church develops leaders with biblical qualifications, it begins to create an environment for ministry within the fellowship of the church.

4

Networking God's People for Ministry

We ought always to thank God for you, brothers, and rightly so, because your faith is growing more and more, and the love every one of you has for each other is increasing. (2 Thessalonians 1:3)

Facing the Dilemma

Once the leadership has drafted the mission statement and philosophy of ministry, the next step is communication. The people in the church need to be apprised of the ministry opportunities. Ideally, a church would have 100% of its members involved, but a more realistic goal is to have 70% to 80% of the members committed to ministry. However, the vision is to see the members serving not only the church, but also the wider community.

As previously stated, a pastor's workload may be overwhelming at times. A pastor must prioritize what he must do each month, week, and day. He must realize that his life will be invaded by crises, emergencies, interruptions, and many other demands upon his ministry and time. He will consistently struggle with time management, deadlines, administrative needs, conflict, and so on. He needs to handle the demands by delegating duties to others or run the risk of burnout by trying to do it all. The predicament of balancing his ministry between studying, praying, and sermon preparation, as well as spending time getting to know his people and their needs, will always be before him. To add to this dilemma, many pastors have forfeited personal time with their families and have lived to regret it. In addition to the church calendar that dictates a pastor's time, there are counseling concerns that also demand his attention. Depending on the pastor, the level of involvement in counseling could be overwhelming. Some pastors gravitate to counseling and end up putting in hours during the week meeting with people. However, there are pastors who shy away from involving themselves in counseling. They may have a personal sense of inadequacy as counselors and conclude that counseling takes too much time and effort, without seeing much improvement in those whom they counsel. Many pastors are more comfortable referring their people to professional counselors.

Counseling and Discipleship

Discipleship is an important aspect of a pastor's church duties. A pastor must recognize that counseling in the church is undertaken in the context of discipleship. This context is best accomplished through an environment of the body of Christ where each member contributes through the caring ministry of one another. The leadership of a church must understand this purpose when establishing a counseling ministry. Counseling involves problem solving; dealing with marital and family issues; addressing sinful behavior; overcoming addictions; and dealing with emotional problems, serious health concerns, and events that create traumatic crises. Counseling should be viewed as helping people to grow and mature in Christ within a loving, caring, supportive, and accepting body of believers. If this concept does not permeate throughout the entire body of believers, then a counseling ministry will not be very successful. Paul wrote a great testimonial to the Thessalonians who were doing this very ministry, stating in 2 Thessalonians 1:3: *We ought always to thank God for you, brothers, and rightly so, because your faith is growing more and more, and the love every one of you has for each other is increasing.* Hendriksen wrote, "The reason for the constant thanksgiving is that the faith of the Thessalonians is growing beyond measure or very much, and that the love of each single brother is constantly increasing, which was exactly what Paul had wished and prayed for so earnestly" (1987, p. 154).

In speaking to his disciples, Jesus gave a commandment in John 13:34, 35: *A new commandment I give you: Love one another. As I have loved you, so you must love one another. All men will know that you are my disciples if you love one another.* To love is to seek the highest good for another individual. This, as Paul wrote, should be the picture of the church.

The people of the church are to understand that their service to the Lord should come out of love, not from obligation or duty. Rather, it should be a ministry in which, as servants, they are motivated to edify and serve one another. A pastor could help build this mindset in the church by leading a biblical study of the "one anothers" to his people. The one-another topics may include love, accept, edify, do not judge, bear one another's burdens, be kind and compassionate, forgive, honor, pray, counsel, be devoted, speak truthfully, encourage, commend, restore, and admonish. This is not an exhaustive list, but just a start to be used by the pastor.

The Holy Spirit has gifted each believer. Referring to spiritual gifts, 1 Corinthians 12:11 teaches that *All these* [gifts] *are the work of one in the same Spirit, and he gives them to each man, just as he determines.* The gifts of the Spirit enable the whole body (the body of Christ) to function correctly. Such gifts are supernatural, not self-determined. Peter emphasized this thought by exhorting believers: *Each one should use which ever gift he has received to serve others, faithfully administering God's grace in its various forms. If anyone speaks, he should do it as one speaking the very words of God. If anyone serves, he should do it with the strength God provides, so that in all things God may be praised through Jesus Christ* (1 Peter 4:10, 11).

Such description of the function of the believers should confirm to the leadership and members of the church that God's plan is to equip his people to serve one another. This should encourage everyone that God will use them in some capacity to supply a significant ministry to the body of Christ.

The Scriptural principle of spiritual gifts and the "one anothers" set the foundation for a counseling ministry in the church. A pastor should have confidence in the Spirit to lead God's people to use their spiritual gifts and talents to meet the emotional, relational, and spiritual needs experienced by the body of Christ.

Utilizing the Members

A pastor has a pool of resources for ministry within the church. He may consider doing a comprehensive survey, along with interviewing all those attending or indicating interest, as to how they desire to serve in ministry of the church. The goal of this exercise is to encourage each member to become involved in some aspect of ministry in the church as well as in the community. This survey and interview exercise will be very valuable for both the leadership and the people of the church. This process will inform the leadership of ways to effectively utilize people in ministry. Another possible benefit of this process is that people will feel encouraged that the leaders of the church desire to have them personally engaged in serving the church and community.

Conducting surveys and interviews is just the beginning of getting members involved in ministry. For the efforts to be effective, there must be follow-through. The leadership must recognize that much of the discipleship and counseling in the local church is done informally. People having very little formal training for ministry may serve the Lord as willing workers in a variety of church programs. Such ministries reflect a healthy church made up of many people voluntarily giving their time, talents, and gifts as loving contributions in service for the Lord.

When the leadership observes people display a caring spirit as they minister, such people should become candidates to be considered for an informal counseling role. The following examples are personal illustrations of how God used church members in voluntary, informal counseling.

Caring Couples

When people face difficult situations, they normally contact the church for help. As pastor, I would meet with them and listen to their concerns. For example, I met with and listened to the heartache of a couple whose son was going through a divorce. The couple was hurt and troubled that their son and daughter-in-law would not seek help in dealing with their problems. They felt helpless and that things were out of control. People in these circumstances often seek their pastor's advice, and I could have offered my counsel; however, I did more than just counsel them. I invited them to our home, along with two other couples from our church who had been through similar experiences. My wife and I, along with the two other couples, ministered to the hurting parents. The other two couples empathized with them, shared Scripture, prayed, cried, and comforted them. The two couples committed themselves to be available any time; they were available day or night for the hurting parents to call upon, and they would be there for them. In this small gathering, I observed the way the church should function. The beauty of the evening was the beginning of close relationships among three couples who were ministering one to another.

A Family Crisis

Another example of networking people in ministry came when I received a phone call from the director of our state church camp. He informed me that one of our junior high girls had confided to her cabin counselor that she was being sexually abused by her father. I told the director that I would report it to the authorities and would work with the family. Arrangements were made for a police officer (who happened to be in our church) to meet with the girl to verify the facts of her testimony. I also had the mother come to my office and informed her of the serious matter between her daughter and her husband. The officer, my wife, and I met briefly with the mother. Sadly, the father was arrested and removed from the home. I realized early on how this would impact the family. The mother was devastated, and the news was very difficult for the girl's older sister and brother.

The family's financial situation was in disarray due to the father being on disability and the mother's income coming from a cashiering job. She was not knowledgeable about handling a budget or paying bills. With her permission, I began to network people in the church to assist this family. I contacted a church member who was a financial advisor for help and informed him about the family's situation. I explained to him that the mother needed assistance regarding her finances. I also explained that he should always take his wife with him each time he went to the mother's home, to avoid any appearance of impropriety. He followed my instructions and reported to me how he was assisting her with her financial situation. He indicated that bills were in shoeboxes in a closet, and she was overdue with the bank and creditors. He put a plan together for a monthly budget and personally called the bank and creditors to communicate her situation and his plan for payment. Fortunately, they all appreciated his call and the plan he had developed. No late fees were assessed, and the bank cooperated with him and his plan. The financial advisor's wife observed that the house had dirty clothes on the floor, unwashed dishes in the sink, and general disarray throughout the house. The mother worked many hours at her job and seemed to not have energy to keep up with the household responsibilities. With the mother's permission, we asked two to three ladies to visit her and help with basic cleaning. The mother called to thank me and stated, "I've never had anyone from the church in my home, and I appreciated their assistance and fellowship."

As the news about this family was known to those in the church, I received a call from a lady from our church who said to me, "I've been praying about this family, especially for the girl who had been abused and for her older sister who was impacted seriously with the information." Furthermore, she informed me that she was a social worker, and her thesis for her master's degree had concerned sexual abuse. She was a godly woman and desired to help the daughters. What a blessing she was in reaching out to help the two sisters! The brother, who was on the high school football team, was dealing with anger toward his father and the accompanying embarrassment. The high school football coach called me and shared that he was concerned for the boy and wondered if he could help the boy work through his struggles. The coach and his wife had started attending our church about a month before the situation became public. I met with the coach and discussed ways he could help the boy deal with his emotional pain and anger.

A testimonial to our church's involvement with this family came from the social services department in the county, which told the court they were very pleased with the work that our church was doing for this family. This became a good report for our church to the community. I invited a board member to assist me as we visited the county jail to meet with the father. In court, I was called to explain what had been done to minister to a family whose lives had been turned upside down. The judge commended me for our church's work in helping a hurting family.

I gave each person basic instructions regarding his or her involvement. Each had a significant role in ministering to this family. While the volunteers of our church were ministering to the family, others were committed to supporting them in prayer.

The mother acknowledged that without the church's help, she didn't know how she would have survived. Satan was out to destroy this family, but God salvaged it, and, out of the ash heap, God received glory through the efforts of godly people who cared.

I remember when I received that phone call from the camp director. My first thought was, "What am I going to do and how will this affect our church? Will it bring discouragement and embarrassment? Will the people step up and shine like lights in darkness and become the church it is called to be?" Praise God, the church shone admirably!

Brotherly Love

When a believer can tell his story, he is ready to counsel people in everyday life situations. Those who have experienced God's healing in life will be sensitive to the needs of others.

I received a phone call from the jailer in town who informed me that a church member had just been admitted and had requested a visit from me as his pastor. Under the influence of alcohol, the man had rolled his car and been arrested for driving while intoxicated. I gave John, a member of our church, a call and asked if he was available to go with me to visit a friend from our church. I explained that we were going to the county jail to meet with a man from church who had just been arrested for driving under the influence. I reminded John, who was a little puzzled as to why he was going along, that when he gave his testimony at church, he had shared how he was saved from a life of alcoholism. I told John that this young man in jail needed to hear his story. As we entered the meeting room, I noticed how scared and frightened the young man was. The accident truly was a wake-up call for him. He knew he had a drinking problem, and he was worried about job security and how his wife would respond to this news.

During the visit, I asked John to share his testimony as to how Christ had worked in his life and helped him to overcome his alcohol problem. Humbly, John empathized with the young man and told his story. The young man listened intently. The young man confessed his sin, and indicated he needed God's help to deliver him from his alcohol addiction. I shared with him that as a church we loved him and wanted to help him. Both men had children who came to our mid-week children's program. I suggested that when they brought their children to the children's program, they should meet during that time and have a Bible study and prayer time together. Week upon week thereafter, I observed these two men going to a room with their Bibles to study and share their lives with each other. Through the accountability and relationship between these two men, the young man began to grow in the Lord. This process contributed toward his healing and led to recovery from and victory over his addiction. It also strengthened his marriage and family relationships. A great byproduct was two men who became close and encouraged one another for several years.

Community Outreach

Two members of our church, a lawyer and a doctor, made an appointment to meet with me. They desired to begin a community Bible study with business and professional men in town. We prayed together for this new ministry that would be led by these men. I helped them in finding Bible study resources for consideration. They launched their first Bible study with six men. In time, it developed into two groups, and then progressed to five separate Bible study groups that met weekly in our town. These two busy professional men volunteered their time to be used by God to reach other men in the community for Christ. Not only were they successful through the Bible study groups, but their efforts also opened doors for informal counseling of the men who attended the Bible studies.

During my years in the pastorate, I had the privilege of serving in the communities as chaplain for a community college, fire/police departments, and a state prison. Such ministries were an extension of our local church. These ministries gave exposure to our church and each one provided many opportunities to do counseling. Our church considered this a win/win for both church and community.

After His resurrection and before His ascension to heaven, Jesus taught His disciples what the role of the church should be, saying, *But you shall receive power when the Holy Spirit comes on you; and you will be my witnesses in Jerusalem, and in all Judea and Samaria, and to the ends of the earth* (Acts 1:8). Although ministry happens through programs of the church, ministry is personal and begins with one's story. It is the personal story of Christ's redemptive work that transforms one's life. This story is told informally and voluntarily. One's story leads to opportunity after opportunity to minister in the church and outside of the church by the power of the Holy Spirit.

I have observed over the years that the church often places people in positions just to fill those positions. This can be a serious error. The church must assign the right people to the right ministry, and then provide training to help them be effective in that ministry. In every ministry, counseling seems to be an important aspect of that ministry.

In the previous examples, God's people ministered to one another without having had formal training in counseling. They became available, faithful servants who offered their expertise, and experiences in life, from servants' hearts. When networking God's people to become involved as caregivers, a pastor must know his people. He needs to know the resources that God has provided in the body of Christ. He should use the resources of his people to their full potential. God did not intend for the pastor to do the entire ministry to the flock, but rather to network the people of God in assisting the leadership to meet the needs of others.

Final Thoughts

The biblical structure represents Christ as the Head of the church, leaders as pluralistic servants to prepare people for ministry, and members of the body of Christ as growing, maturing, edifying, and discipling one another. God's model of the church creates the proper environment and climate for such a ministry. Without this model, counseling loses its uniqueness as a natural byproduct of a caring, loving community.

5

Recruiting the Counseling Team

Since we have gifts that differ according to the grace given to us, each of us is to exercise them accordingly.... (Romans 12:6, NASB)

Spiritual gifts are given by the Holy Spirit to be exercised by the members of the body of Christ. They are supernatural in nature. Such gifts may be related to one's talents to accomplish the work of the Lord. Someone may have a great musical talent, yet this talent may never be used to minister to others. Spiritual gifts given by the Holy Spirit are confirmed by others in ministering to them. Therefore, gifts are always related to ministry. Paul describes this principle in 1 Corinthians 12:4–6: *There are different kinds of gifts, but the same Spirit. There are different kinds of service, but the same Lord. There are different kinds of working, but the same God works all of them in all men.*

Over the years, there has been a focus on spiritual gifts in the church. Some in the church have concluded that if they don't have a certain spiritual gift, they can't or won't serve. Others have not considered how God might use them in helping people identify their spiritual gifts, so they may benefit others. It might be practical advice to encourage church members that the reason they are given a gift is to benefit the church, rather than seeking a gift for personal gratification. Notice what Peter wrote to the believers: *Each one should use whatever gift he has received to serve others, faithfully administering God's grace in its various forms. If anyone speaks, he should do it as one speaking the very words of God. If anyone serves, he should do it with the strength God provides, so that in all things God may be praised through Jesus Christ* (1 Peter 4:10, 11). Note: More will be said on this subject in chapter 8, "The Game Changer."

Because the pastor and leadership of the church are to equip the saints (God's people) for works of service (Ephesians 4:11, 12), it stands to reason that teaching and training will be a major aspect of their ministry. Vincent wrote, "The omission of the article from teachers seems to indicate that pastors and teachers are included under one class. The two belong together. No man is fit to be a pastor who cannot teach, and the teacher needs the knowledge which pastoral experience gives" (1924, p. 390). This appears to indicate that the pastor was both shepherd (caregiver) and teacher (training and equipping). It should also be noted that Paul uses the plural tense, signifying multiple types of leadership in shepherding and teaching.

If pastors are negligent in fulfilling their role as teachers and shepherds, the ministry of the church will suffer. There seems to be a universal principle that weak church leaders produce weak churches. Similarly, weak fathers will produce weak families and weak CEOs will produce weak entities in the corporate world. Leadership has the responsibility to make it their priority to train those who are under their influence.

When we look at the life of Jesus, we see the calling of His twelve disciples. Of the twelve, three of the disciples—Peter, James, and John—were part of His inner circle. Jesus spent more time with them than with the other disciples and confided in them His relationship with His Father and His purpose on earth as the Messiah. The next group was the other members of the twelve whom Jesus taught and explained what it meant to *come, follow me, and I will make you fishers of men* (Matthew 4:19). A wider circle of followers outside the twelve were considered disciples in a broader sense. They followed Jesus and listened to His teaching, watched Him perform miracles, and observed Him as He moved amongst the common people. This outer circle of disciples varied in their understanding of and commitment to following Jesus.

Church Structure for Counseling

In the local church, there is an arrangement similar to Jesus' ministry on earth. The core group of disciples is be the leadership of the church. This would be the pastor and staff, as well as the church elders. They have the responsibility of leading, discipling, and teaching members and attendees of the church. The next circle is men and women who serve in ministry roles, such as teachers, children and youth leaders, adult ministries, counseling, and the like. It is paramount that people in these positions receive teaching, training, and mentoring.

The pastoral staff must spend much time in teaching, leading, and discipling the inner circle who are part of the plurality of leadership. This approach involves constantly dealing with issues, questions, and problems faced by leaders who need guidance while doing ministry. The exchange of concerns and the interaction with the leaders and the pastoral staff provides application of the Word of God as it relates to the issues presented. Leaders increasingly develop confidence in themselves and in the Scriptures to fulfill the call of God upon their lives. Through this training process, the leaders become effective servants.

Recruiting the Right People as Counselors

A counseling ministry through the church should begin slowly. Church leadership must be supported, and the pastor must communicate clearly what a counseling ministry entails and how it will function.

The first step is to develop a small team of believers to assist in the counseling needs of the church. To start with, the counseling team should be no more than six to ten people comprised of couples and singles. Over time, the team may grow in numbers according to the size of the church. This team should be comprised of mature believers, persons who are knowledgeable in the Word and are respected by others. These believers, through life experiences, should be able to articulate the application of the Scriptures to the problems people face today. Their temperaments should reflect gentle, humble, and teachable spirits. Ephesians 4:1, 2 is clear: *As a prisoner for the Lord, then, I urge you to live a life worthy of the calling you have received. Be completely humble and gentle; be patient, bearing with one another in love.* This group must also understand the importance of confidentiality and accountability as they work with people. Their lives must be lives of integrity.

Characteristics of Counselors

Because they are dealing with other people's lives, team members must be grounded in the Scriptures as the source of hope and change. They must have a respectable understanding of theology and its relevance to life, along with a biblical methodology for the counseling process. A pastor will want his team to rely upon using the Bible in counseling and be able to navigate comfortably through the Bible while helping others as they seek biblical solutions for problems. It has often been said that a pastor's wife could make or break his ministry. This is true of a counseling team as well. Not having the right people in place could create a lack of trust that may seriously damage the church. The recruiting of the counseling team must be a priority and a matter of prayer.

Other characteristics of team members are important, too. Church leaders must find people who are available. The counseling team must be ready to meet with those in need and commit themselves to counseling over time. People are more comfortable meeting with others who are likeable and approachable. Showing interest in others is a valuable trait. Philippians 2:3, 4 support the type of person who can be used effectively in a counseling ministry: *Do nothing out of selfish ambition or vain conceit, but in humility consider others better than yourselves. Each of you should look not only to your own interests, but also to the interests of others.* Another necessary characteristic of a counselor is a spirit of gentleness. Because counseling can be very tense and stressful, patience, gentleness, and self-control are vital for any counselor. Scripture speaks to this characteristic: *Brethren, even if anyone is caught in any trespass, you who are spiritual, restore such a one in a spirit of gentleness; each one looking to yourself, so that you too will not be tempted. Bear one another's burdens, and thereby fulfill the law of Christ* (Galatians 6:1, 2).

Lastly, it has been mentioned before but must be stressed again: the counseling team must have confidence in using the Bible as the basis of their counseling ministry. The members of the counseling team must have an uncompromising conviction that the Scriptures are true and reliable.

The importance of God's truth is paramount in having confidence in one's counseling ministry. This is illustrated by the music student who asked his professor, "What can we know for sure?" The professor took a tuning fork and struck it. He then declared to the student, "That is an 'A.' It will always be an 'A.' Every instrument adjusts to the 'A' in getting tuned. The piano may be out of tune and the soprano in the other room may be off-key, but the tuning fork is always accurate, pure, and true." This reminds us that the Bible is always accurate, pure, and true, and the final authoritative source for truth. Psalm 19:7–8 states, *The law of the Lord is perfect, restoring the soul. The testimony of the Lord is sure, making wise the simple. The precepts of the Lord are right, giving joy to the heart. The commands of the Lord are radiant, giving light to the eyes.*

In his letter to the Ephesians, Paul makes the point that the counselor should regard everything in life as it relates to the love of Christ. *I pray that out of his glorious riches he may strengthen you with power through his spirit in your inner being, so that Christ may dwell in your hearts through faith. And I pray that you, being rooted and established in love, may have power together with all the saints, to grasp how wide and long and high and deep is the love of Christ, and to know this love that surpasses knowledge that you may be filled to the measure of all the fullness of God* (Ephesians 3:16–19).

A counselee who is facing problems, troubles, and difficulties is often overwhelmed and has difficulty making sense of anything. Life is often like a puzzle, as one deals with fragmented pieces from one's emotional, physical, social, mental, and spiritual behavior. God understands and has provided for humanity the answers found in the Bible. The process of assisting in restoration of humanity to its intended purpose and giving sense to the puzzle of life is included in the work of a counselor. Puzzles come in a box with the picture of the puzzle on the box cover to help in putting it together. A counselor will constantly refer to the picture of humanity found in the Bible to bring about biblical change in the life of a counselee. There is no greater calling for a counselor than to assist counselees through the Bible to find the solution to their problems.

When the leadership recruits a counseling team that demonstrates the fruit of the Spirit; displays characteristics of integrity, faithfulness, and humbleness; and is respected and above reproach, then that team is ready to provide training to others to assist them in the counseling process.

6

Training the Counseling Team

You then, my son, be strong in the grace that is in Christ Jesus.

And the things you have heard me say in the presence of many witnesses entrust to reliable men who will also be qualified to teach others.
(2 Timothy 1:1, 2)

The leaders' role consists of training others. They are to equip godly people to counsel one another. This will involve understanding the biblical constitution of humanity. The trainee must realize that counseling is not a quick fix. It involves the process of sanctifying people by helping them understand the patterns in thinking, attitude, and behavior that must be changed for God's glory.

The purpose of a leadership and counseling team is to come alongside others to urge, implore, or persuade. 1 Thessalonians 5:11 and 14 describe this approach: *Therefore encourage one another and build each other up, just as in fact you are doing …. And we urge you, brothers, warn those who are idle, encourage the timid, help the weak, be patient with everyone.*

Counseling teams are made up of godly people with a desire to help others who are facing problems. They are willing to be taught and trained to be effective caregivers and counselors. They acknowledge that helping others is a serious task and should not be taken lightly, so they recognize the need for proper guidance and help from the pastoral staff. Therefore, it is also important for the leadership team of a church to have good training resources in theology and counseling (see Appendix B).

Counseling the Unbeliever

Biblical counseling focuses primarily on counseling Christians. However, a counselor will have the opportunity to counsel unbelievers as well. The priority for the counselor in that instance would be to present the gospel of Jesus Christ clearly, with the intent and prayer that the counselee would respond to the message and by faith believe on the Lord Jesus Christ as Savior. Paul clearly reminds believers: *For by grace you have been saved through faith; and that not of yourselves, it is the gift of God; not as a result of works, so that no one may boast* (Ephesians 2:8, 9, NASB). A counselor must communicate to an unbeliever that the counsel will be ineffective in the long term if the unbeliever lacks the spiritual strength and power given by the Holy Spirit to overcome his or her problems. A biblical counselor can give good advice in the areas of better communication skills, proper approaches in dealing with conflict, financial principles to live by, and so on. However, if a counselee does not know the Lord, he or she will be unable to persevere with biblical application. Scripture clarifies this truth in 1 Corinthians 2:14: *The man without the Spirit does not accept the things that come from the Spirit of God, for they are foolishness to him, and he cannot understand them, because they are spiritually discerned.* Hopefully, the counselee will become a believer, and then the counselor's responsibility will be to disciple the new believer.

Counseling the Spiritual Believer

When counseling Christians, a biblical counselor must distinguish between a spiritual and a carnal believer. In 1 Corinthians 2:11–15, the Apostle Paul describes the characteristics of those who are spiritual. First, the Spirit of God resides within them (v. 11): *For who among men knows the thoughts of a man except the man's spirit within him? In the same way no one knows the thoughts of God except the Spirit of God.* Second, those who are spiritual have a desire to know the Word of God (v. 13): *This is what we speak, not in words taught us by human wisdom but in words taught by the Spirit, expressing spiritual truths in spiritual words.* The third characteristic, found in Galatians 5:22, is that the spiritual life reflects the fruit of the Spirit: *But the fruit of the Spirit is love, joy, peace, patience, kindness, goodness, faithfulness, gentleness and self-control.* Paul explains that the fruit of the Spirit is observed by those *who live by the Spirit and you will not carry out the desire of the flesh* (v. 16). A spiritual individual lives by the Spirit, walks by the Spirit, is guided by the Spirit, is taught by the Spirit, and is controlled by the Spirit. A spiritual believer responds to the command, in Ephesians 5:18, to be *filled* [controlled] *by the Spirit.*

This is not to say that a mature believer does not need counseling. Believers are always on a spiritual journey. This journey consists of all the spiritual highs and lows experienced throughout life. Spiritual growth is ongoing, and an active work of God in the life of a believer.

A counselor's goal in counseling is to move a counselee toward restoration. *Brothers, if someone is caught in a sin, you who are spiritual should restore him gently* (Galatians 6:1). To "restore" means to repair or to mend. The point is for the counselee to be reinstated into fellowship with God and humanity so the counselee can be useful again in service for the Lord. The result of this process brings glory to God.

The Carnal Believer

Many believers are not experiencing Christlike, spiritual life. They are identified by Paul as carnal: *And I, brethren, could not speak to you as to spiritual men, but as to men of the flesh, as to infants in Christ. I gave you milk to drink, not solid food; for you were not yet able to receive it. Indeed, even now you are not yet able, for you are still fleshly…* (1 Corinthians 3:1–3). Paul speaks of the infant (new believer in Christ) as carnal, as well as of one who does not grow in the Lord over time and remains fleshly or worldly. Notice that Paul addresses them as "brethren." A carnal man, whether a new believer or one who has been a believer for some time, is still a Christian. This type of Christian often seeks counseling due to immaturity and lack of wisdom from God. James 1:8 acknowledges that *this man is double-minded, unstable in all he does.*

Characteristics of the Carnal Man

As noted in 1 Corinthians 3:1, 2, a carnal Christian is weak spiritually. Notice Paul's language here: *fleshly, mere infants, I gave you milk, not solid food.* He goes on to describe the nature of a carnal believer in verse 3 (*there is jealousy and quarreling among you*) and describes them as being divisive among the brethren in verse 4 (*one says, I follow Paul, and another, I follow Apollos*). This description indicates that carnal believers continue to operate in the flesh, and as infants, they are immature in their faith. These characteristics reveal that this kind of carnal believer grieves and quenches the Spirit due to sin in his or her life (see Ephesians 4:30 and 1 Thessalonians 5:19).

As a counselor works with a Christian who is an immature, weak believer involved in sinful behavior, the counselor's role becomes that of moving the counselee toward restoration. Note Galatians 6:1: *Brothers, if someone is caught in a sin, you who are spiritual should restore him gently.* To *restore* means to repair or to mend. The point is to be reinstated into fellowship with God and humanity. Once this process is accomplished, the believer can be useful in serving the Lord, which brings glory to God.

An intriguing question that Jesus asked a crippled man at the side of the Bethesda pool where the disabled would gather is described in John 5:2–8:

> *Now there is in Jerusalem near the Sheep Gate a pool, which in Aramaic is called Bethesda and which is surrounded by five*

colonnades. Here a great number of disabled people used to lie—the blind, the lame, and the paralyzed. One who was there had been an invalid for thirty-eight years. When Jesus saw him lying there and learned that he had been in this condition for a long time, he asked him, "Do you want to get well?"

"Sir," the invalid replied, "I have no one to help me into the pool when the water is stirred. While I am trying to get in, someone else goes down ahead of me."

Then Jesus said to him, "Get up! Pick up your mat and walk." At once the man was cured; he picked up his mat and walked.

Bethesda was known as a home of incurables. It was a place of pain and sorrow, wretchedness, and despair. Notice the approach taken by Jesus: He confronted the condition of the man directly by breaking through the barriers of complacency, self-pity, and dejectedness. Further evidence of this man's bondage was seen in an attitude of hopelessness and helplessness. Jesus presented to the man a greater power, the power of the gospel in the person of Himself, Jesus Christ, who could deliver and heal him. Just like the man at the pool, counselees also struggle with sincerely wanting to change.

As a counselor helps a counselee to understand the characteristics of a spiritual and carnal believer, it becomes an encouragement for the counselee to recognize that one can go from being a natural person to a spiritual person and from a carnal person to a spiritual person. One can also go from spiritual to carnal, but one can't go from spiritual or carnal back to a natural person. This was addressed earlier in 1 Corinthians 3:1, which clearly begins with "brothers," a term only used to mean believers.

Notice the order in which Paul leads the reader. First, he emphasizes the spiritual believer (1 Corinthians 2:10–13). He then explains the person without the Spirit, the unbeliever (verse 14). In 3:1–7, he follows by describing the carnal believer. This order appears to be the proper goal for a Christian: Be spiritual, not carnal. This is the intended life for all believers.

Having the Right Motivation to Change

When a counselee seeks counseling to get help with his or her problems, a counselor must explore whether the counselee is sincerely genuine in wanting God's solution. In *Competent to Counsel*, Jay Adams suggests (from his Personal Data Inventory) questions to be asked by the counselor in determining the counselee's issues:

1. What is your problem?

2. What have you done about it?

3. What do you want us to do? (1970, p. 274)

A counselor must recognize erroneous motivations in the answers to these questions, such as seeking happiness, wanting to escape personal responsibility, shifting blame, desiring tranquility and peace, finding justification for fleshly desires, and so on. Scripture states that change takes place in one's heart (motivation) as well as in one's outward expression (behavior). Often a counselor will sympathize with, encourage, and pray with a counselee without confronting the counselee's motives. The outcome often is that after a few weeks of counseling, the counselee has lost interest, is ready to give up, and loses the desire to make biblical change. Regardless of their problems, circumstances, or failures, counselees must understand that their decisions must be motivated by the desire to please God and glorify Him. Any other motivation will be temporary and not grow peace in the heart of an individual. A counselee must accept this and take ownership, which is pleasing to God. Paul shared with the Thessalonian church: *Finally, brothers, we instructed you how to live in order to please God, as in fact you are living* (1 Thessalonians 4:1). Paul also wrote to the church at Colossae, *And we pray in order that you may live a life worthy of the Lord and may please Him in every way: bearing fruit in every good work, growing in the knowledge of God …* (Colossians 1:10). It is evident that both churches were motivated to please the Lord. In pleasing the Lord, a counselee is glorifying God, not self. 1 Corinthians 10:31 reveals this principle: *So whether you eat or drink or whatsoever you do, do it all for the glory of God.* This must be one's motivation, or success in the life of a counselee will be short-lived.

Influences that Affect Change

Once a counselee establishes the correct motive to live by, a counselor begins to probe the counselee in three important areas of influence. These areas of influences are thinking, attitude, and behavior, which are simplified in the acronym T.A.B. Sometimes the letter S is added to the acronym, standing for the word *spiritual* or *sinful*. Spiritual thinking will influence spiritual attitude, which influences one's behavior. However, sinful thinking also influences one's attitude and behavior. A counselor spends much time with a counselee asking questions in these three areas. The questions to use to explore these areas are: who, when, where, and how. Such questions provide data that the counselor will need in guiding a counselee through the counseling process. Without following this process, a counselor may jump to conclusions prematurely. The way a counselee thinks, either spiritually or selfishly, will influence the counselee's attitude, which will in turn influence the counselee's behavior. The selfish way of thinking consists of feelings that influence action or behavior, which influences thinking. The acronym to remember this is F.A.T., which stands for feelings that influence action and thinking. "Feelings" indicates an attitude to do as one feels; followed by "acting," which refers to impulsively reacting according to one's emotions and feelings. "Thinking" comes after the fact, in which a counselee realizes that his or her behavior has created problems and wrong outcomes, escalated emotions, and produced wrong behavior. Counselees eventually begin thinking about their problems remorsefully, which leads to feelings of rejection, resentment, anger, or guilt, while being unable to fix or repair the situation. Counselees are left to face the fact that the problems are beyond their control. Often, counselees will seek help that will satisfy their flesh: basically, someone to sympathize with them. At this point, counselees may seek as counselors, friends whom they can convince and win over to get their support. Fleshly counselees are not interested in taking on personal responsibility, nor humbling themselves, nor asking God to work in their lives.

A counselor must stay focused while working with a counselee where change has to be addressed in proper thinking, attitude, and behavior. The goal is for a counselee to begin to know that one's thinking must be biblical, that one's attitude must be spiritual, and that one's behavior must be godly. This process challenges old thinking patterns, selfish attitudes, and unbiblical behavior. For some, the F.A.T. approach has been the norm for a long time. This approach can be illustrated by a person who has one leg shorter than the other: the limp in walking feels normal due to the long-standing adjustments made by the body. The counseling procedure should take into consideration the deep-seated patterns that have characterized a counselee over the years. Making the proper adjustments in life will seem awkward and uncomfortable. As a counselee begins to practice right thinking, right attitude, and right behavior, new patterns will begin to develop and the spiritual process of being conformed to the image of God's Son escalates (see Romans 8:29).

In *The Counsel of Heaven on Earth* (2006, p. 150), Jones writes about Martin Luther, who followed a personal exercise to help him to extract the precious from the worthless.

1. *Challenge your thoughts. Luther's first step was to challenge his negative, ungodly thinking.* For each destructive thought, he would say, "Das ist nit Christus" ("That is not Christ").

2. *Replace your unhelpful thoughts with godly ones.* After challenging each thought Luther would make a positive affirmation of faith. These affirmations can take a variety of forms, including repeating memorized verses of Scripture, prayer, poems, and statements of faith. In Luther's case, he usually sang a hymn of praise. I like to imagine him loudly singing his own hymn "A Mighty Fortress Is Our God."

It would be beneficial for a counselor to be acquainted with the following Scripture to serve as a guide in helping a counselee:

THINKING—Titus 1:15; Romans 7:23, 8:6, 12:2–3, 16:18; 2 Corinthians 10:5; Philemon 3:19, 4:4–9; 1 Corinthians 1:10

ATTITUDE—Philemon 2:5; Hebrews 4:12; Romans 12:1–2; 1 Peter 4:1; Proverbs 15:15, 30, 28:14

BEHAVIOR—Romans 1; Titus 1:16; Galatians 16–23; Ephesians 4; Colossians 3; Proverbs 4:27

A counselor should focus on a counselee's behavior if such behavior is destructive, before exploring a counselee's thinking and attitude. For instance, if the serious offense by a counselee is anger-driven, which may lead to the counselee harming others, then the priority of change would be to address the behavior. In time, a counselor will move to the areas of thinking and attitude to discern what might be causing the behavior. Changing one's behavior is not, however, the final goal. Keep in mind that a person can change his or her behavior but may do so for the wrong reasons, such as to comply with the counseling in the short term to convince the counselor that change has been made. Change must take place in all three areas of thinking, attitude, and behavior for it to meet the criteria of biblical change.

A Biblical Counseling Process

The training of a counseling team should provide a clear, biblical approach to helping people. The team must be comprised of volunteers who are knowledgeable in the Word, mature in their faith, and have a willing heart to help others to walk with God. Generally, team members are not experienced in counseling others. They need guidance and training with opportunities to gain experience to counsel. The following approach may be helpful in training a counseling team.

The first step in meeting with people is to identify the problem. A counselee may present many issues as to what the problem(s) may be. Often in a counseling session a counselee cannot articulate specifically what the problem is. A counselor must probe the counselee by using an interview process, collecting data from printed forms such as surveys and counseling instruments. (These items are discussed later in this book.)

Once the problem(s) have been identified, the next step by a counselor is to determine if the problem is directly addressed in Scripture. Some issues are clearly identifiable in Scripture, such as cheating, drunkenness, murder, anger, idolatry, and abusive behavior, whereas other problems may not be as clearly addressed. If it's unclear to a counselor, the next step to take is to consider what biblical principle a counselee is violating. For instance, a couple may disagree on the method of parenting their children or have differences in handling conflict or proper ways of managing their finances. The Bible doesn't address these issues specifically. The direction for the counselor is to help the couple to understand the underlying principles. Working through this process is vitally important. A counselor patiently navigates through these steps to verify what the problem or problems are. If counselors simply take the word of a counselee without verification and investigation, they may be totally misinformed and give misguided counsel. A counselor should be ready to go to the next step in seeking the solution to the problem.

Finding, identifying, and knowing the biblical solution to the problem becomes the area where a counselor works with a counselee on understanding and acceptance. A counselor needs to exercise discernment and wisdom as to biblical solutions. A counselee may push back by denying, shifting blame, or challenging the conclusions presented by a counselor. If the counselor has done due diligence in identifying the problem with the biblical solution, then a counselee has a problem with Scripture, not with the counselor. If a counselee accepts the biblical solution given by the counselor, the process continues to the final step, which leads to implementation.

Implementation is the proper application regarding the solution. This step calls for commitment on the part of a counselee to make proper adjustments in thinking, attitude, and behavior. New patterns must replace old patterns. From week to week in the counseling process, accountability between counselor and counselee is paramount. Encouragement on the part of a counselor when the proper adjustments are made will reinforce the choices that are biblically correct. Confronting a counselee over negligence to follow through in making the right decisions will be crucial as well. Such confrontation must be done with the right spirit. A counselee may be fragile, weak, and easily discouraged. How a counselor responds to a counselee will many times determine the outcome. Ephesians 4:2 speaks to this subject: *Be completely humble and gentle; be patient, bearing with one another with love.* If a counselor doesn't have this spirit, the counseling could be disastrous. A counselor's method is as crucial as the truth presented to a counselee.

The training of a counseling team should involve role-playing counseling situations using the method described here until this procedure becomes natural in working through issues that people face.

Resources to Enable Spiritual Growth

A counselee should be informed of the God-given resources that will enable spiritual growth. It is only the believer who has the advantage of applying God's resources for long-term success. 1 John 5:3–4 communicates this principle: *This is love for God: to obey his commands. And his commands are not burdensome, for everyone born of God has overcome the world. This is the victory that has overcome the world, even our faith.* At each session, a counselor might go through a checklist to hold a counselee accountable in applying the resources offered by God to facilitate growth. There are many resources that could be shared, but the following five have been used effectively in counseling.

The Power of Prayer. Ultimately, it must be understood that the solution is found in God and His Word, not in a counselor or self-help remedies or other worldly resources. Prayer works in the heart and will of each human to help bring about obedience to God. Prayer strengthens the faith of the weak. Prayer leads to a reliance on God and waits patiently on Him and begins to accept God's plan for one's life. Through prayer, one begins to trust God with one's problems and trust Him with the outcome. Ultimately, prayer recognizes that God's way is the right way and brings the believer to pray as Christ prayed: *Not my will but thine be done* (Luke 22:42).

The Spirit of God. The promise Christ gave to His disciples was that He would not abandon them. Instead, He would send them a comforter. Jesus encouraged His disciples by saying, *But when He, the Spirit of truth, comes, He will guide you into all truth* (John 16:13). Also supporting this passage is 2 Corinthians 1:21–22: *Now it is God who makes both us and you stand firm in Christ. He anointed us, set his seal of ownership* *on us, and put his Spirit in our hearts as a deposit, guaranteeing what is to come.*

The Word of God. A counselee needs to develop and maintain confidence that the Word of God is sufficient, that it can be trusted and is reliable in all matters of life. This resource is God's blueprint for successful living (Psalm 19:7–11; 2 Timothy 3:16).

The Family of God. It is a great privilege to belong to the "family." God's family is all those who have put their faith in Jesus Christ as their Savior. This is called the *universal church*, in which the family is literally around the world. In this family is a kinship of the spirit, a commonality in the faith, and a fellowship that is unique from other relationships. The believer draws encouragement and edification from others in the family of God. The familiar song by the Gaithers is so true, "I'm So Glad I'm a Part of the Family of God." What a blessed resource!

The Local Church. This refers to the assembly of believers in a local community. In this assembly, teaching, discipleship, fellowship, and serving provide an environment for the believer to mature in the Lord.

Hebrews 10:24–25 reads: *And let us consider how we may spur one another on toward love and good deeds. Let us not give up meeting together, as some are in the habit of doing, but let us encourage one another—and all the more as you see the Day approaching.* I have had Christians come for counseling and asked them what church they attend. Many shared that they were not attending any church. It may be that they haven't attended church for several years. I work with them in finding a Bible-believing church as part of their growth project.

If a counselee neglects one or more of the resources, the results will certainly hamper victory over personal problems.

A Counselor's Prayer

A student at our seminary desiring to be a biblical counselor presented me with a personal prayer she hoped to live by as a biblical counselor.

> I pray that the Holy Spirit would give a counselor the ability to discern the thinking and behavior of a counselee that God wants to change. May the Holy Spirit reveal God's Word that is needed in changing the thinking and behavior that is desired by God.
>
> It is my prayer as a counselor that the goals set by me for a counselee would be for the glory of God. May I not endorse unbiblical thinking, attitude, or behavior, but would encourage a counselee toward biblical standards and morals.
>
> May I impress upon a counselee that I continually rely upon the Holy Spirit and God's Word in asking discerning, insightful, and clear-to-the-point questions to properly ascertain what the problems are and the solutions to those problems. I also pray that the Holy Spirit will grant me, as a counselor, strength that will not allow feelings to control the decisions and/or advice given to a counselee. By God's grace, may I always follow divine wisdom and lead a counselee to experience the abundant life as promised by Jesus Christ.

May this prayer echo in all our hearts in agreement, as we strive to be biblical counselors.

The next chapter, chapter 7, builds on the counseling foundation and describes the "game changer" that brings about the proper outcome for a counselee: the gospel of grace, growth projects, and personal responsibility.

7

Guidelines for Using God's Truth in Counseling

Blessed is the man who does not walk in the counsel of the wicked or stand in the way of sinners or sit in the seat of mockers. But his delight is in the law of the Lord, and on his law he meditates day and night. (Psalms 1:1, 2)

This book is not a textbook on biblical studies or methods of understanding biblical interpretation. However, it certainly would be valuable for a pastor to communicate to his team some fundamentals related to understanding biblical text and its application. The average person in a church may even have taught Sunday school or led a Bible study group, yet never had teaching on the fundamentals of biblical interpretation. Church leaders assume too much about their people's ability to use the Bible accurately.

What does one need to know to venture into an arena with Bible in hand, ready to assist another regarding a solution to problems that is drawn from the Word of God? A counselor should be aware of various pitfalls that should be avoided in biblical counseling. For counselors to say they are biblical because they use Scripture is not necessarily accurate. The misuse of Scripture may be very misleading and damaging to a counselee. A counseling team should be aware of inappropriate methods of biblical interpretation.

CHAPTER 7

What a Counselor Should Avoid

A counselor must avoid using the method of self-interpretation. This pitfall is illustrated by a counselor who reads a passage from the Bible and asks the counselee, "What does the Scripture say to you or what does it mean to you?" This approach bypasses important steps in understanding the original passage and moves directly to application, which is self-interpretation. This method leaves the meaning of the text up for grabs and can be misleading for a counselee. A counselor may fall into the temptation of listening to a counselee, quickly turning to a passage of Scripture, and then asking the counselee, "How does this passage apply to your present need? What does it say to you?" This is called *proof texting*, where the counselor or counselee reads a passage at random to find the solution to a problem. Criticism against the biblical counseling method is often aimed at this approach—and rightly so.

Related to the self-interpretation approach is the use of Scripture as a quick fix, in which a counselor is anxious to turn immediately to the Word and admonish a counselee. Often when counselors use this approach, they have not sought enough information from a counselee, nor have the counselors taken the time to listen to the counselees to establish the total picture of the problem. This approach uses Scripture to excuse a counselor from properly diagnosing the issues related to the problem. Scripture is used as a placebo. A counselor may read passages of Scripture, say a prayer, and send a counselee off—only to have the counselee become disillusioned, disappointed, and perhaps have second thoughts about the validity of biblical counseling.

Scripture is not a magical, mystical technique where a counselor learns a prescribed method to cure the soul. Methods of repeatedly praying a passage of Scripture, reciting and repeating Scripture until a breakthrough occurs, or claiming a biblical promise(s) as one's own, all in the name of Scriptural counseling, is not using God's Word appropriately for counseling. This name-it-and-claim-it method becomes a mystical, mechanical system that is shallow and misleading because it is not genuinely Scriptural. However, this is not to say that memorizing Scripture, singing Scripture, or quoting Scripture should be avoided.

A counselee may attend counseling sessions with the motive to seek success, happiness, change in relationships, wealth, health, and many other self-driven reasons, and in these cases Scripture is viewed as a self-help tool. This approach ignores the whole counsel of God, isolates what a counselee is seeking, and builds a system or procedure to gain a desired end. When this approach is implemented, it ignores and leaves out much of the biblical message and isolates itself from or insulates itself against certain aspects of doctrine and behavior that may cause a counselee to be uncomfortable and not politically correct. It tends to pick and choose what will make a counselee happy, fulfilled, or successful rather than seeking to produce a godly and holy life.

Another approach to avoid is interpreting Scripture by spiritualizing or interpreting Scripture allegorically. A counselor using this method seeks to look beyond the literal meaning of Scripture to a deeper or secondary meaning. Such a counselor interprets the Scripture apart from its grammatical, historical meaning and identifies a hidden meaning as the only important factor of the text. Scripture is to be interpreted literally unless the passage clearly carries a spiritual/metaphorical meaning. An example is Revelation 3:20: *Here I am! I stand at the door and knock. If anyone hears my voice and opens the door, I will go in and eat with him, and he with me.* This verse is often used by counselors to refer to the heart of man, where Jesus is knocking at the door of the heart wanting to be admitted. The meaning of the text is Jesus standing at the door of the church in Laodicea, where he is outside of the fellowship of the church, and knocking because He wants in. A strong component of biblical counseling should be that of teaching the Word of God. Many professional Christian counselors have been trained in counseling techniques, methodology, and theory with very little biblical and doctrinal background. Therefore, Scripture is used on the surface in a supportive role rather than as the primary function of the counseling procedure.

There are a variety of instruments related to temperament techniques and analysis where Scripture is considered for support. Examples are Tim LaHaye's books, *Spirit-Controlled Temperament* (1967) and *Transformed Temperament* (1971); Meier, Minirth, and Wichern's *Introduction to Psychology and Counseling* (1982, pp. 385–392), where they describe personality traits in marriage, and Dan and Kate Montgomery's book *Compass Psychotheology* (2006, pp. 3–19). These instruments are used to show traits, patterns, and characteristics of a person's personality and temperament. Interpretation of the instruments is subjective, rather than objective, which leaves room for error. Many of these instruments exist, but they are similar in nature, with minor variations and applications. They may be interesting and helpful as one identifies certain personality traits and recognizes how those traits reflect an individual temperament, which can further relate to the person's behavioral patterns. However, temperament analyses do not take into consideration one's change in environment, stresses in life, impact on relationships, careers, and so on. To be labeled as a particular personality type may minimize the work of the Holy Spirit in changing a person's life.

I've read Christian authors who write about biblical characters as having certain dominant personality types, and others who give certain animal-name associations as temperament identification. There's an old saying "Make the main thing, the main thing." Can understanding their personality makeup help people? Yes, to a point. Should it be the main thing? No.

At one point, a couple came to me for marital counseling. They were working through their differences and communication styles. Their church had a seminar on a popular temperament theory and at the beginning of one of our counseling sessions the husband spoke up and declared, "I learned at church why we don't get along! It is my temperament style which is... and her style is... and she wants me to change. That's my style and I'm not going to change!" This attitude set us back in the counseling procedure. I recognized that the husband was using the study on temperaments as an excuse for his behavior and that he wasn't interested in genuine change. My point here is to serve as a warning and encourage counselors to be very cautious in using these instruments. I have heard that some pastors will go so far as not marrying couples based on their temperament differences.

Proper Guidelines

After learning and considering what a counselor should avoid, counselors need to identify areas to apply in biblical interpretation. The first question to ask in reading the text of Scripture is: What was the intended message from the author to those who first heard or read his words? This step helps counselors understand the historical context of the passage they are using with a counselee. A biblical statement may have numerous applications but has only one correct meaning or interpretation. Put another way, there is one interpretation but many applications. The original meaning of the text by the author should be the priority of a counselor.

The next step for a counselor is to focus on the grammatical aspects of Scripture. The Bible was written in Hebrew, Aramaic, and Greek. It was written in these languages not because God preferred these languages as spiritual, but because they were the languages of the people at the time it was written. A counselor could go astray if the historical/grammatical approach is ignored. Some pastors teach New Testament Greek to their people, which is a real advantage to their church members and those considering counseling. Many churches do not receive such an opportunity; therefore, they need to know about various resources that will assist a serious student of the Word. A source that is helpful for a counselor is Jacobs's *Power Sword Discovery Bible New Testament with God's Power Promises* (1987). A counselor should seek to understand the context of a given passage by being alert to what precedes and what follows a specific thought by the author. Counselors will also seek to acquaint themselves with how the passage might be used by the author in other writings. The more one knows of the context of the whole, the better understanding one has in interpreting the Scriptures.

The next approach in interpreting Scripture is to follow the literal interpretation of Scripture. This approach is the logical, natural method to use. The natural meaning of a passage is to be interpreted according to the natural rules of grammar (poetry, apocalyptic material, letters, parables, etc.), syntax (putting together sentences, clauses, etc.), speech, and context. This approach avoids the temptation to spiritualize a meaning from the text to fit a counselee's situation.

An area that is often overlooked in understanding Scripture is examination of the cultural and geographical background of the text. The political and socio-religious life during biblical times should also be examined. The life and times of biblical history occurred in the context of culture and various traditions. The cultural traditions may not dictate to the reader application for today, so the reader must inquire if the text is stated as a command to be followed (and to whom the command was addressed). Religious, cultural, and geographical differences will help the reader understand what the text is stating. For instance, John 4 describes Jesus going to Samaria and speaking to a woman at the well. An understanding of the attitudes that Jews and Samaritans had toward each other would be valuable. The historical background of this text, such as differences in their religions, would bring clarity to an understanding of the text. Gender issues related to Jesus speaking to this woman will play a part in further comprehending the cultural, historical, socioeconomic, religious, geographical, and ethnic elements of the text.

A *descriptive* passage is just that: it describes the events that the author wishes to communicate. A *prescriptive* passage gives God's normative truth that He desires people to know and obey. This is illustrated in 1 Corinthians 9:1–25, where Paul describes the fact that he is single and that he and Barnabas work for a living. This passage is not a mandate for all who are in ministry to remain single and support themselves by working. Paul acknowledges that he has a right to have a wife and to be supported in ministry, yet he forgoes such rights (vv. 14–18). In verses 24–25, he challenges readers (prescriptive) to recognize that we're all runners in a race and we should run in such a way as to get the prize. Notice verse 25, which reads: *Everyone who competes in the games goes into strict training. They do it to get a crown that will not last; but we do it to get a crown that will last forever.*

For a counselor, an important consideration of Scripture has to do with the application of the text. Such questions could include, but not be limited to: How does this work? Or, so what? How can I relate this information in a relative way to a counselee? What should a counselee do once he or she understands the meaning of the text? What should I do about it?

Scripture demands a response by the reader. A counselor communicates Scripture with proper commands, advice, and biblical principles. A counselee's choice is to both submit and be obedient to the Scriptures or to deny, neglect, and turn away from Scripture's admonition. Hebrews 4:12 (NASB) states: *The Word of God is living and active. Sharper than any double-edged sword and piercing as far as the division of soul and spirit, of both joints and marrow, and able to judge the thoughts and intentions of the heart.* The Word of God brings conviction to the heart of a counselee. It is to the Word that counselees are accountable. A counselor should allow the Word, not the opinions of humans, to be the authoritative and final word. The Bible is not a reference book of options, suggestions, and recommendations; it does not allow a take-it-or-leave-it approach. Counselees must grapple with what God is saying and if they disagree, their issue is not with the counselor, but with God.

A biblical counselor relates to a counselee with the intention and desire to assist that counselee to be all he or she can be in the Lord. In view of Psalm 37:3–5, a counselor encourages counselees to apply the biblical truth to their lives. *Trust in the Lord and do good; Dwell in the land and cultivate faithfulness. Delight yourself in the Lord; and He will give you the desires of your heart. Commit your way to the Lord, trust also in Him, and He will do it* (NKJV).

When counselees meet with a counselor, they are coming with problems. These problems create discouragement and many times confusion. The faith of counselees, and their trust in God, become weak. A counselor is aware of the emotional condition of counselees and how their perspectives have affected their lives. A counselor serves as a **facilitator** in guiding a counselee through the maze of difficulties and leads a counselee to the cross of Christ where there is grace, mercy, and love. At the cross, both counselor and counselee are on the same plane as sinners before God, in need of a Savior. A biblical counselor comes alongside of a counselee and shares how the work of Christ on the cross provides healing and hope. As a facilitator, a counselor strives to assist a counselee to move toward reconciliation both to God and humanity. *Therefore, if anyone is in Christ, he is a new creation; the* *old has gone, the new has come! All this is from God, who reconciled us to himself through Christ and gave us the ministry of reconciliation* (2 Corinthians 5:17–19, NASB).

In addition to being a facilitator, a counselor serves as a **coach**. This is done through leading, teaching, and guiding counselees in the way of righteousness. A counselor's office should include a white board, computer, or other teaching tool so the counselor can give visual teaching illustrations related to the life of a counselee. A counselor is a teacher and an encourager, demonstrating patience, humility, and gentleness in sharing God's plan for living. The method of redemption is offered at the cross. Jesus spoke words of hope in John 16:33 (NASB): *These things I have spoken to you, so that in Me you may have peace. In the world, you have tribulation, but take courage; I have overcome the world.*

The task of a counselor is to point counselees to their solutions through Jesus Christ. As a coach, a counselor is not to sympathize with a counselee and lose sight of the goal in counseling, which is to guide the counselee toward the solution. This leads to victory and avoids using counseling sessions to wallow in despair, focusing on the past and offering no lasting hope.

A counselor serves as a **mentor**, which is a role like coaching. *Webster's New World Dictionary* defines *counselor* as a "wise, loyal advisor, teacher or coach." Mentor usually refers to a model person, experienced in his or her field or area of expertise. A mentor is someone to pattern one's life after, someone to follow, and someone to consider it a privilege to learn from. Young Timothy attended diligently to what Paul said and did. He observed Paul's character, morals, integrity, and values. Paul lived his life with purpose, faith, and perseverance, serving as a mentor to Timothy. Paul did not isolate himself from Timothy; rather, he lived out his life before the young apprentice. In Philippians 4:9 Paul wrote, *whatever you have learned or received or heard from me, or seen in me, put it into practice.*

Paul was authentic, approachable, and available. This is the life of a mentor. However, some professional counselors live in an ivory tower isolated from their clients. In private practice, this type of counselor is often impersonal and unengaged. This is not the case with biblical counseling in the context of the church.

One distinction of biblical counseling is that it is **relational**. It happens in an environment of a local church where people care for and know and trust one another. They have a faith and doctrine they all adhere to. They are available for one another and desire that members of the family of the church truly experience life, joy, and peace from God. They are diligent to pray for, share hospitality with, and counsel one another. It doesn't get any better than this; no other system or program apart from the church can be its equal.

Bible Versions and Translations

If your church has a preference or choice of a Bible translation to be used, it would be helpful for counselors to follow suit and

A senior executive of a large bank had risen to a place of prominence and influence, but he had started as an office boy. The president of the company said to him, "I want you to come into my office and be with me each day." The executive's reply to this request was, "What could I do to help you, sir? I don't know anything about finances." The president replied, "With me you will learn what I want to teach you a lot faster if you just stay by my side and keep your eyes and ears open." This executive concluded, "That was the most significant experience of my life. Being with that wise man made me just like him. I began to do things the way he did and that accounts for what I am today." This is mentoring!

use what is familiar in that church. The question is often asked, "What translation is best to use in counseling?" People certainly can get confused when they see so many versions and translations on the market today. Rather than describing all of them, with their strengths and weaknesses, here I focus on only one question: What's best to use in counseling? My practice has been to use the New International Version (NIV) published in 1978, which is a phrase-for-phrase translation. It is simple to read and easy to understand. I often ask a counselee to read from the NIV in a counseling session and to discuss the verse(s) read. The other translation I recommend is the New American Standard Bible (NASB). This is a very good word-for-word translation. It too is easy to read, but not as wordy as the NIV.

As I stated earlier, use the Bible that is primarily used in your church. This will be most familiar for those in that congregation. You may also want to discuss this with your pastor. The last thing a counselor needs to do in a counseling setting is to offend someone over what Bible version is used. My comments are suggestions, not dictations, as to what you should use.

Confidence and Relevance

A counselor has the great privilege of sitting down with hurting people and opening the "bread of life" to them. Biblical counseling has been described as one beggar going to another beggar and telling him where to find bread. The Bible is dynamic and powerful, and by observation, interpretation, and application can change the course of one's life. The late Dr. Howard Hendricks of Dallas Theological Seminary would often say, "The Bible was not written to satisfy your curiosity; it was written to transform your life."

The late Dr. R. C. Sproul (author and theologian) was hired to teach in a Christian school. The president of the school said to him, "We need someone young and exciting, someone with a

dynamic method who will be able to make the Bible come alive."
His reply? "You want me to make the Bible come alive? I didn't
know it had died. In fact, I never even heard it was ill. Who was
the attending physician? No, I can't make the Bible come alive
for anyone. The Bible is already alive. It makes me come alive. My
prayer is that through my futile attempt I make in helping others
to know the Scriptures, that it will make others come alive."

8

The Game Changer

If you love me you will obey what I command. And I will ask the Father, and he will give you another Counselor to be with you forever — the Spirit of truth. (John 14:15, 16)

A biblical counselor does not rely on his or her insight, wisdom, or knowledge alone in helping others. Psalm 32:8 relates the words of God: *I will instruct you and teach you in the way which you should go; I will counsel you with My eye upon you.* The theme running through this book is to rely on the Holy Spirit throughout the counseling process. This chapter underscores this necessity and continues to develop the biblical method of counseling.

A counselee, who by faith believed in the work of Christ on the cross on his behalf, received a new nature by the regenerating work of the Holy Spirit. At salvation, the individual was baptized by the Holy Spirit. This baptism placed the believer in the body of Christ. 1 Corinthians 12:13 (NASB) states, *For by one Spirit we were all baptized into one body, whether Jews or Greeks, whether slaves or free, and we were all made to drink of one Spirit.* Also, at salvation the believer was indwelt by the Spirit. In Ephesians 3:16–17 (NASB), Paul prayed for the saints at Ephesus *that he would grant you, according to the riches of his glory, to be strengthened with power through his Spirit in the inner man, so that Christ may dwell in your hearts through faith.* Then Paul declares, in verses 20–21, *Now to him who is able to do far more abundantly beyond all that we ask or think, according to the power that works within us, to him be the glory in the church and in Christ Jesus to all generations forever and forever. Amen.* This blessed hope of having the Holy Spirit involved in all aspects of the counselee's life should bring reassurance that help is available and imminent.

The Holy Spirit Is the Counselee's Counselor

The game changer for believers is the work of grace in receiving the power of the Holy Spirit to overcome problems in their lives and for each to live a godly life with a desire to do the will of God. But it doesn't stop there. The Holy Spirit continues to work in the life of the believer by teaching, guiding, filling, assuring, equipping with spiritual gifts for service, and praying for the believer. One's confidence in the work of the Spirit in one's life should give certainty and hope that no issue or no problem will leave the believer paralyzed or helpless, nor forever left in bondage. Paul states, in Romans 8:2 (NASB), *For the law of the Spirit of life in Christ has set you free from the law of sin and of death.* Counselees need confidence in relying on the Holy Spirit to be their counselor in problem solving. They need to realize that their victory is in Christ, and this victory ultimately should bring honor and glory to Christ alone, not to the counselee or the counselor.

The work of the Holy Spirit involves the work of sanctification in the life of the believer. Sanctification is the process of becoming Christ-like in all matters of faith, practice, and attitude (Ephesians 5:18). *Also, we, who with unveiled faces all reflect the Lord's glory, are being transformed into his likeness with ever-increasing glory, which comes from the Lord, who is the Spirit* (Romans 3:18, NASB). The believer is "set apart from sin" unto Christ. When Paul addressed the church in Philippi, he spoke to them corporately, referring to the saints, saying, *For I am confident of this very thing, that he who began a good work in you* [plural] *will perfect it until the day of Christ Jesus* (Philippians 1:6, NASB). The Scriptural application certainly carries the principle of the individual believer in whom God is working (sanctifying the believer) in a progressive manner.

Why is this the game changer? Because this gift—of the Holy Spirit to every believer—provides the solution to every need. Those outside of Christ have only willpower, which is short-lived. Temporal solutions often weaken the will of humans and bring about discouragement. Those outside of Christ (nonbelievers) do not possess the Holy Spirit, so they are left with no divine help, power, or hope. The counselor needs to drive home this thought. Counselees need to trust God, rely on the Word of God, and look to the power of God that is offered immediately to aid and assist them. The biblical counselor encourages the believer by explaining that the believer has a great advantage over those without the Spirit, for God has provided His Spirit to enable the counselee to experience victory.

It should not come as a surprise to a counselor when a counselee gives lip service expressing a need for God's help, but at the same time limits God's ability due to the magnitude of the problem. People often feel such guilt that they place themselves outside of God's love, mercy, and forgiveness. They become so absorbed with their problems that they wonder if God can really help them. The Apostle Paul gave a personal testimony in 1 Corinthians 12:9 when he was suffering with a thorn in the flesh. He pleaded with God three times for the Lord to take it away: *But he said to me, my grace is sufficient for you, for my power is made perfect in weakness.* Then, in 10:13 (NASB), Paul wrote, *No temptation has seized you except what is common to man. And God is faithful: he will not let you be tempted beyond what you can bear. But when you are tempted, he will also provide a way out so that you can stand up under it.* A counselor needs to underscore these Scriptures and others to give a counselee hope and confidence that God is able and willing to provide strength and power for the counselee to be an overcomer.

As stated, sanctification by the Holy Spirit is a progressive matter. There are highs and lows in life as one is being conformed to the likeness of Christ (Romans 8:29). As counselees are obedient to

Christ and His Word, they are being filled (controlled) by the Spirit (Ephesians 5:18).

Paul set forth a procedure when he wrote in Ephesians and Colossians regarding a two-step process for change. This process is identified as to "put off and put on," described throughout the Bible. In the biblical counseling field, this is a major guide in helping counselees. Much has been written to demonstrate its effectiveness in working with people. The following example helps to explain this approach.

The Two-Step Process Illustrated

A husband and wife came for counseling and began to share their problems. The wife spoke first. "My husband has a bad habit. In public, he constantly criticizes and denigrates me." Her husband countered by saying, "It's no big deal, I'm only joking." His wife looked at him and explained, "It's hurtful; I'm uncomfortable with it in public and I've asked you to stop speaking like that in front of others."

As the counselor communicates the "put off and put on" process to the husband, the husband is encouraged to follow step one, "putting off." The husband turns to his wife, takes on the responsibility, and says to her, "I have ignored your plea to stop criticizing you in public and I am sorry. I guess I didn't take you seriously as to how it affected you that way. Will you forgive me?"

The counselor shares step two with the husband. This step moves from "putting off" to "putting on." The biblical solution for step two is found in Ephesians 4:29, which challenges the believer, *Do not let any unwholesome talk come out of your mouths, but only what is helpful for building others up according to their needs, that it may benefit those who listen.* The counselor encourages the husband to practice this two-step approach, asking his wife for forgiveness and asking God, by His Spirit, to help him to have victory concerning the way he speaks of his wife in public. The counselor has the husband read 1 Peter 3:7: *Husbands, in the same way be considerate as you live with your wives and treat them with respect as the weaker partner and as heirs with you of the gracious gift of life, so that nothing will hinder your prayers.*

The husband has fulfilled step one, the "putting off" of disrespectful speech. He continues to speak to his wife, "Honey, I have done more than hurt you. I have disobeyed God and His Word. Forgive me for being insensitive to your needs and not listening to you. I will begin to show respect and speak kindly of you from now on."

In step two, the husband must learn discipline by "putting on" kindness as mentioned in Colossians 3:12: *as God's chosen people, wholly and dearly loved, clothe yourselves with compassion, kindness, humility, gentleness and patience.* The husband must develop new patterns to replace old patterns. Works of the flesh must be replaced by the works of the Spirit (Galatians 5:19–26).

As the husband applies Ephesians 4:29, a plan of these two steps should become clear as to what he must do to honor and respect his wife. He must begin thinking of her out of respect. He should develop an attitude of respect and speak of her in public from a heart of goodness and kindness in his behavior. Verse 29 indicates, in step one, that *no unwholesome talk [is to] come out of your mouth.* The husband begins to "put off" words that put his wife down and degrade her through his speech. In applying step two, he uses words that are helpful for building her up. Therefore, his conversation is to edify his wife before others. This process begins to display his spiritual/Scriptural obedience. Such behavior is not only recognized by his wife in the way he speaks of her in public, but also, as verse 29 states, benefits others who are listening. The husband begins to grow in the Lord in his journey in life under the sanctifying process. The husband must break old habits and practice the new habits of speaking respectfully to his wife at home. The more the right habit is developed through his speaking in normal circumstances, the easier it will become to speak respectfully in public. The counselor may stress to the husband to consider Ephesians 5:25–33, by pointing out the fact that he is showing love for his wife as Christ loves the church.

Another consideration in helping the husband would be for the husband to ask his wife to remind him in a gentle and kind way when he violates the biblical principle of speaking respectfully. Her response should not be, "There you go again, will you ever change?" She is to encourage him and assist him as he grows in the Lord in this area. The sanctifying process is a lifelong journey of personal spiritual growth. The counselor may encourage the husband to do a Bible study on Ephesians 6:10–18, addressing the believer who is to put on the whole armor of God.

In George Mueller's autobiography (1984), he stated that he disclaims having the gift of faith, but explains that his faith "is the same faith which is found in every believer, and the growth of which I am most sensible of to myself; for by little and little it has been increasing for the last sixty-nine years" (p. 17). This is a clear understanding of the process of sanctification in one's life.

Growth Projects

A distinctive part of counseling is the use of homework. Homework is assigned to a counselee each week to work on between counseling sessions in order to accelerate the counselee's growth process. Earlier in this book I mentioned that I use the term "growth projects" instead of the word "homework." When used consistently as a tool in the counseling procedure, growth projects will speed up the counseling process. Growth projects serve as measurable indicators for the counselor to determine how committed counselees are in seeking solutions to their problems. Growth projects determine the counselees' sincerity and desire to commit themselves toward change. The growth projects also serve to keep counselees focused on the Scriptural solution rather than the counselor.

Practical Projects

As stated earlier, there are two types of growth projects. The first type is "practical growth" projects. This name refers to assigning a counselee practical actions and steps that assist the counselee in personal accountability, which will help in developing better relationships between the counselee and others. In marital counseling, it might be practical advice to encourage the husband to take personal responsibility for doing chores around the house without being asked, or to hold his wife's hand when they go on a walk, and so on. Another practical step for a couple would be to establish the habit of communicating to one another by saying "I love you" a few times a week to the spouse. A couple may set a time to meet together weekly to share and discuss issues related to their everyday lives. Practical growth projects will put action into the relationships, which will reinforce to the recipient that the counselee is truly desirous of meeting the needs of others. *Each of you should look not only to your own interests, but also to the interests of others* (Philippians 2:4).

A couple met with me for counseling and immediately the wife indicated her frustration with her husband. I asked her to explain the facts to me. She said her husband just didn't help her with anything around the house. I asked for an illustration. "Well, the other day I came home from the grocery store and unloaded the car myself. Trip after trip I walked right past him with groceries as he was sitting in his easy chair watching television. After I carried all the groceries in the house, I looked at him and said, 'Couldn't you help me carry the groceries in from the car? I walked past you time after time and you just sat there as if I didn't exist.'" I asked the husband if he remembered the incident and how he had responded. He acknowledged that he did remember but said that he had been totally involved in a game on TV and just didn't realize she was making the trips into the house with the groceries. She broke into the conversation and said to me, "This is what I deal with all the time." I asked her why she didn't go to him and request help with unloading groceries from the car before she started taking the groceries out of the car. Her response was, "How could he not know that I needed help when I walked past him all those times?" I turned the attention back to the husband: "It appears that you seem oblivious at times when your wife could use your help." He agreed that he hasn't been much help and fails many times in this area. I asked him to seek his wife's forgiveness and desire to assist her in the future. I then said to the wife that due to his habitual negligence, she had developed a pattern of setting him up for failure by waiting for him to not respond and then pointing out his neglect. "You need his forgiveness for your failure in asking ahead of time for his assistance." They both confessed their sin to each other.

The growth project for the coming week was for her to ask her husband when she needed help, in a kind way. For the husband, the project was to acknowledge the request and respond by helping her. They both agreed they would try it. The next week they came in and said it had worked. The wife was surprised that he put forth the effort and the husband was pleased that he didn't get chewed out for not responding.

Habits, however, will take time to establish. Every week during the counseling process I would ask them if they were continuing to follow through on the projects. It wasn't always perfect for them, but as the weeks transpired it became the norm for them.

Academic Projects
The second type is called "academic growth" projects. This may include a number of different assignments: reading material related to the counselee's problems; Bible studies; taking sermon notes on Sundays; Scripture memorization; and/or topical biblical

worksheets in the area of struggle (such as anger, addiction, depression, temptation, sexual sins, holding grudges, selfishness, or forgiveness, to name a few). As the counselor lays out a plan to assist counselees in dealing with their problem(s), academic growth projects will play a major role in that plan.

A counselee must recognize that growth project assignments are given for the counselee's good: they are not just busy work or ways to please the counselor. The counselor should stress the importance of fulfilling the assignments shortly after the session, and not waiting until just before the next week's appointment. This allows the counselee a week to apply and learn the value of the project, and to consider whether it was helpful and beneficial. The counselor must recognize that many counselees are not used to this procedure in counseling; nevertheless, after one or two sessions the counselee should be following through with the projects and will appreciate the effectiveness of the process. The counselor must stress the importance of growth projects in every session, indicating that they are a vital aspect of assisting counselees in their growth. (For sample growth projects, see Appendix C.)

I had a couple call for counseling and say that they desired to come as soon as possible to get help. At our first session, I explained the purpose of growth projects and stated that I expected them to fulfill the requirements from week to week. They quickly agreed that they would work on the projects. At the next session I asked them to pull out the growth project and report on how well it went. They indicated that the week had been very hectic and said they didn't have time to do it. I again stressed the importance of growth projects to them and asked them to fulfill the assignments shortly after the counseling session. The next week, to my disappointment, I received the same report as the first session: they hadn't done the projects. I smiled, then asked them to go to a room that had a table and chairs and asked them to do the academic worksheets together. I said that when they finished, they could meet with me and we would go over them. They were paying for the counseling sessions and realized they were paying for part of the session to do their growth projects. This communicated to them that I considered growth projects to be very important. After that session they never missed doing their growth projects again.

An individual came to me for biblical counseling after a year of secular counseling and having received an expensive counseling bill per session. After she experienced the biblical counseling procedure, she shared that she had never received any outside work assignments from her previous counselor. The growth projects enabled her to focus on her problems and learn how she could apply biblical solutions to them.

Keeping the Balance

A counselor needs to keep a balance between the practical and academic growth projects. Encouragement should be given at each session for the counselee to bring a report along with the academic projects, to see how the counselee is progressing. The beginning of each session should be dedicated to discussing the application of the projects and their effectiveness. From week to week, both the counselor and the counselee evaluate the plan and its benefits. Growth is the goal. Growth projects become the method.

The counselor must use discernment as to what projects will work for a particular counselee. Some will gravitate to the academic projects, working on reading material and doing worksheets, whereas others will drag their feet in doing projects like that. Immediately the counselor has a problem: one party is well prepared, while the other party feels guilty for not keeping up. The counselor must make growth projects a win for all parties involved. Discernment seeks to find the right balance, so all parties are encouraged to keep moving forward. As the counselor observes strengths and weaknesses through growth projects, the counselor continues to adjust the assignments that will work best for the counselee.

As an example, consider the husband who showed disrespect to his wife by his speech. The counselor may give growth projects to assist him to "put off and put on," such as:

- Practice speaking respectfully to his wife at home. The more the right habit is developed through his speaking in normal circumstances, the easier it will become to speak respectfully in public. This is a practical growth project to be carried on during the week.

- For the academic project, have the husband read and memorize Ephesians 4:29, *Do not let any unwholesome talk come out of your mouths, but only what is helpful for building others up according to their needs that it may benefit those who listen.* Another verse to memorize would be 1 Peter 3:7: *Husbands, in the same way be considerate as you live with your wives, and treat them with respect as the weaker partner and as heirs with you of the gracious gift of life, so that nothing will hinder your prayers.*

It is important at each session for the counselor to go over the assignments and to encourage counselees when they complete and fulfill the growth projects. This reinforces the purpose of growth projects and motivates the counselees to continue the process. In counseling the exemplar couple, the wife was asked how her husband was doing with his growth project. Her reply was very positive; she stated how proud she was of his progress in speaking and showing respect to her. The husband smiled and reached over and hugged her. The three of us rejoiced together and I prayed with them and thanked the Lord as to how their relationship was growing.

9

Counseling Considerations

May the God who gives endurance and encouragement give you a spirit of unity among yourselves as you follow Christ Jesus, so that with one heart and mouth you may glorify the God and Father of our Lord Jesus Christ.

Accept one another, then, just as Christ accepted you, in order to bring praise to God. (Romans 15:5–7)

In his book *Faithful Feelings* (2006), Elliot underscores the proper relationship of church members with one another. He writes,

> How we love each other has everything to do with how we feel about one another. Love will draw us into fellowship. In an era of churches focusing on professional, state of the art presentations and great music, perhaps some of our churches need to revive the potluck dinner, family night, and church picnics. The church family has the most wonderful reasons to rejoice; joy and laughter should characterize our fellowship together. We are called to enjoy one another's company just as Jesus made best friends. It is only in loving and enjoying one another up close that we will be prepared to bear one another's burdens when the pain and crises of the world come rushing upon us. (p. 266)

A church climate such as the one described here helps to facilitate a counseling ministry in a fellowship of closeness and openness among the family. Setting this foundation in the fellowship communicates a sincere concern for one another that enables a credible ongoing counseling ministry.

Starting the Process

A local church might have the congregation or leadership of the church consider how people might fulfill the one-another ministry. An excellent starting point would be to study the "one anothers" in Scripture. There are more than thirty Scriptural passages of "one anothers," but a sample list to consider includes: love one another, accept one another, edify one another, bear one another's burdens, serve one another, be kind and compassionate to one another, honor one another, and forgive one another. The church leadership may use this tool in leading group discussion to assess what the church should implement to become better equipped as a ministry-driven church. Once the vision of the church is set by the leadership, and the counseling team is in place and training has begun, it is time to consider practical observations regarding counseling.

Practical Advice in Counseling

Most church members are reluctant to serve as counselors in their church, due to lack of experience and wondering if they are qualified to do counseling. This is understandable and must be addressed by the leadership in the training process. The following material is helpful, practical advice for laymen to consider if they think they might desire to be counselors.

When counseling others, <u>do not assume anything</u>. Counselors must withhold any conclusions or judgments until they are confident that all the facts have been collected. An example is the counselor speaking to one spouse about marital issues and then drawing conclusions and prejudging the issue without ever speaking to the other spouse. Proverbs 18:17 states, *The first to present his case seems right until another comes forward and questions him.* Collecting data may take a while. People often withhold 40% of information from a counselor due to fear or uncertainty as to whether they can trust the counselor with such information.

The biblical counselor should <u>integrate prayer throughout the counseling procedure</u>. Prayer is given at the beginning and at the close of a session, but it should not be restricted to that. Prayer is appropriate when the counselor senses it is needed throughout the session. When a breakthrough happens in an issue, it is appropriate to pray and praise God for what He has done. This also signals to the counselee the importance of prayer and its place in the life of a believer. The counselor recognizes that prayer may be the healing balm needed at that time in the session.

The counselor must <u>develop the skill of listening</u>. It takes self-discipline to listen and not interrupt the counselee by inserting what the counselor wants to share or point out. Listening can be exhausting and mentally draining. The counselor's artful listening speaks volumes to counselees that they are being respected and heard, instead of being lectured by the counselor.

A suggestion for the counseling team is to split into groups, discuss a topic, and practice listening to other members while working on not interrupting each other. This exercise should be practiced at home with family members and in other settings to develop listening skills as part of the counselor's communication style. As the counselor practices the skill of listening in life situations, the more natural it becomes as part of the counseling experience.

The novice counselor often is tempted to try to resolve all problems in one session. This attitude attempts to plant, water, and harvest all in one session. It rarely works that way. A typical approach in counseling is to have between eight to twelve sessions. Therefore, the counselor prioritizes which problems should be dealt with first, second, and so on until all issues have been addressed and resolved. It is suggested that the counselor focus on one issue at a time, starting with an issue that is simpler to resolve. This procedure instills confidence in the counselees: if the counselor can help in one area, perhaps she or he may be able to help with success in the difficult areas. The counselor is to <u>be an agent of hope</u>. By moving from session to session, the counselee begins to develop confidence and hope in the counseling process.

The counselor is to <u>develop a personal involvement with the counselee</u>. This is accomplished by communicating a sincere interest in the counselee. The counselor commits to helping the counselee as a brother or sister in the Lord. This relationship demonstrates personal involvement that displays transparency, a spirit of coming alongside the counselee with biblical truth given through love and compassion. The counselor has a conviction, and desire, to see a brother or sister experience peace, joy, and love in the Lord. Counseling is to assist the counselee to be restored, reconciled, and walk in the Spirit. The biblical counselor is convinced that God's Word is truth and as counselees apply the biblical resources to their lives, change will begin to take place.

Another necessity for the counselor is to <u>practice proper communication skills</u>. Communication is extremely important in the counseling process. This is not the place to use theological jargon or words to impress counselees. The counselor learns to articulate in succinct, short sentences, avoiding that which is difficult to understand. If you can communicate your position clearly enough for a child to understand it, you have learned to communicate well. <u>Communicating biblical truth</u> is the primary task and call of the counselor.

At the end of the session, the counselor <u>uses appropriate growth projects</u>. Homework assignments were covered in chapter 8, but some practical matters should be considered. The counselor should stress that the projects are for the counselee's benefit. It will be to the counselee's advantage to begin working on the growth projects within two days after the session. The counselee should be assigned from three to five projects per week. A balance between academic and nonacademic projects is suggested.

In some cases, such as severe depression, memory loss, hearing voices, loss of energy, disorientation, unusual sleep disruptions, and the like, it may be wise for the counselee to see a medical doctor. A doctor may be able to determine whether the symptoms are due to emotional or physical reasons.

Another tip for the counselor is to <u>always counsel those of the same gender</u>. It should be male to male and female to female. Team counseling, with one male and one female, would be appropriate in counseling persons of the opposite gender as well as in counseling couples.

Another consideration is for the counselor to <u>respect the counselee's time</u>. The counselor should not waste the counselee's time with undue or lengthy conversation at the start of a session. Be punctual and be in control by guiding the sessions toward proper goals and objectives. Graciously direct and tactfully stay on track, bringing counselees back to the topic at hand if they begin to ramble. Remember, when counselees are nervous, upset, or frustrated, they often tend to talk more and faster than usual.

A pastor once said to me that he will spend up to four hours at a time counseling people. This is unnecessary and at the end simply disrespects both parties' time. Counselees will take advantage of the counselor's time if this is allowed. Some counselees view counseling as talk therapy, and it stops there. The counselor prioritizes issues to cover and sticks to it for that session, knowing that other issues will be covered in another session.

Those who are beginners in counseling are often so concerned about doing well that they develop a messiah complex. This is the attitude in which a counselor takes on more responsibility than necessary in doing all he or she can to fix the problem. The overeager counselor begins to play God in the life of the counselee by taking on and usurping the role of the Holy Spirit. Such attitudes will lead to burnout and failure.

The counselor would be well advised to <u>use resources</u> such as other Christians, pastoral staff, and prayer partners to support the counselor's efforts. However, the counselee must approve such recruitment by the counselor, to protect confidentiality. This sharing also avoids personal pride on the part of the counselor when the outcome is successful. The counselor also appreciates the value of the body of Christ that may complement the counselor's efforts in accomplishing the end results.

It is advised that the counselor guide the counselee toward <u>making commitments</u> that lead to proper changes. Each counseling session moves toward commitment. Change is the goal. To seek change, counselees must understand their sacrifice and investment regarding personal responsibility for change. The counselee must clearly understand the steps that must be taken to move closer to the solution of the problem. Such commitment should be measurable, so both the counselor and counselee can identify progress in achieving the goals. Steps of commitment create accountability between counselor and counselee. The counselor uses these steps of commitment to encourage and motivate the counselee to keep pressing forward. At the end of the session, counselees should be able to articulate changes made and how the counseling is assisting them in personal life changes.

Making commitment is difficult. Making lasting commitment is desired. Counselors should not conclude that they have succeeded during the early stages of counseling. Counselees may make commitments early on to please the counselor, but those commitments may not be lasting. Perseverance is needed. A false assumption as to the counselee's commitment by the counselor may put the counseling process in jeopardy.

The <u>proper use of time invested in counseling</u> by the counselor must be monitored. If the counselor is investing more time and energy than the counselee, it is time to confront the counselee. Counselees may appear to be serious and wish to work through their problems. However, when the problems aren't resolved right away, they lose their motivation. The counselee must realize the importance of making it a priority to persevere and to take personal responsibility for putting forth the effort. A key indicator that reflects a breakdown of the counselee's commitment is neglect of the growth projects. Also, if counselees are going through a crisis, they will tend to run to a counselor for a "quick fix." When the crisis lessens, the counselee loses the urgency to invest in the counseling procedure.

An Illustration of Counselor/Counselee Time Imbalance

I received an urgent phone call from a couple indicating that they must meet with me as soon as possible. I made time for them in my schedule. In the first session, I listened to their concern about their marriage and immediately began to give them hope and encouraged them to begin working on steps, through growth projects, that would assist them and move them toward a resolution. I asked them to work on the assignments during the week and be prepared to discuss what they learned from the growth projects. They assured me they would do so. During the week I spent several hours searching the Scriptures and other counseling resources, along with prayer on their behalf, so I would be prepared to work with this couple who so desperately needed my help. To my dismay, when we met for the second session, they had not done anything I had requested them to do. Instead, they offered excuses about not having time due to other activities in their lives.

From my counseling experience, I must say that this spirit by counselees is not an exception to the rule. Counselor, do not allow your investment to be greater than that of the counselees. By doing so, you're enabling them to fail and then they will blame you for their lack of success. The counselee must understand that commitment, along with time investment and accountability, is crucial for counseling to be successful.

Another word of advice for the counselor is <u>to observe the counselee's body language</u>. Body language often is an indicator of how the counselee is responding in a counseling session. The counselor should be observant of the counselee's eye movements, facial expressions, posture, voice fluctuation, and hand/body movements throughout the session. It is helpful for the counselor at times to ask the counselee to describe the body language, rather than risk misinterpreting or misreading it. This feedback from the counselee regarding body language avoids misunderstanding or misinterpreting the counselee. Therefore, the counselor must not rely on body language alone as the criteria for judging the counselee. A key principle for the counselor is to have counselees interpret and verify their bodily responses.

An Example of Wrong Intentions

A couple came for marital help. During the first session, they seemed to be serious in wanting to work on their marriage. The husband brought his Bible to the sessions and seemed to be compliant for the first few sessions. Shortly thereafter, it became clear that the husband's motivation for coming was to make his wife change, not himself, and that he thought if she changed the counseling would have been successful. The counselor confronted the husband about his contribution toward the breakdown in the marriage and abruptly he left the counseling office, wanting nothing to do with counseling. He attended counseling with the wrong motivation and as a result it revealed his heart condition after three sessions. Appearance is not what it always appears to be. His marriage ended due to his pride and stubbornness.

As people in the church begin counseling, they desire to help people, yet at times they face personal defeat and failure. The counselor must recognize that what happens in the counseling session is a matter of timing. If the counselee's heart is not ready for godly counsel, not much can be accomplished. Remember, the Holy Spirit is not through with the counselees even if they quit the counseling process. People may walk out, and it may take them a year before they return to seriously address their problems. Counselors should, however, always <u>review and evaluate their approach and procedure</u>, as a counselor, to determine if something they might have done caused the counselee to abort the counseling process. The counselor must be objective and honest in this assessment. The counselor is to be faithful to the Lord in helping people. With approval from the counselee, counselors may share their concerns with the leadership for proper input and supervision as to what adjustments might be made to improve the counseling if possible. Remember, the Lord is the one who works in the hearts of humans in drawing them to Himself through the Holy Spirit. If the heart of a person is hardened and unwilling to submit to godly advice, ultimately that becomes the counselee's problem, not the counselor's.

Each counseling case is unique and different from those of the past. Therefore, the counselor <u>should not rely on past successes</u> for present victories. Do not become lazy and rely on experience alone. Constantly be learning, reading, and staying up with various issues people face. Stay in the Word, research counseling problems, and be on the growing edge. Do not allow personality, techniques, knowledge, and experience to be the beginning of pride before the fall.

<u>Never minimize the nature of the problem</u> presented by the counselee; always take the counselee seriously according to the counselee's own assessment. The counselor may think that common sense would yield a logical answer to the problem and wonder why the counselee can't see this solution to the problem. However, problems for people many times create confusion, illogical thinking, and bad judgment. A principle to remember in counseling is that an event plus time equals distortion. Often, the counselee can't see the trees for the forest. It is the counselor

who brings logic, stability, objectivity, and common sense to the counseling process.

It is appropriate to <u>use illustrations</u>, whether personal or from past counseling experiences, in helping counselees to better understand their problems. A word of caution for the counselor: Counselees may associate the illustration with someone in the church or another counselee and wonder if they too will be used as an illustration in the future. The counselee may also misinterpret the illustration, which could potentially do damage and lead to a wrong conclusion.

Discernment is important when the counselor uses personal illustrations with counselees. The focus could be too much on the counselor and may actually distract the counselee. This may sound like people are paranoid, but when they are going through counseling issues, they have a tendency toward reading into things. Pray for discernment as to what should be shared through illustrations. A great resource for illustrations is the Bible. There are approximately 2,900 people in the Bible. Many Bible stories make for good human-interest illustrations. Know biblical characters and what they faced in going through the journey of life.

From session to session, the counselor should <u>monitor the counselee's spiritual condition</u>. The counselor will notice indicators in the life of the counselee that may represent a biblical change in the counselee's thinking, attitude, and behavior. The Christian life is a continuous process of character maturation and development in knowledge and understanding of the Word and work of God in one's life. When the fruit of the Spirit begins to appear in the life of the counselee, the counselor is reassured that biblical counseling can be used to help bring about such spiritual change. Is the counselee moving from the milk of the Word to the meat? Does the counselee apply the Word of God to life issues? Is there a desire by the counselee to do all things, words, and deeds for the glory of God? Is there a sensitivity by counselees to personal sin, and do they move to correct it through confessing sin to the Lord and others against whom they have sinned? Is there a genuine willingness and desire to grow and walk with the Lord? If the counselor senses a positive improvement regarding these questions, it may verify other indicators of spiritual growth.

Biblical counseling generally is conducted with those who profess to be believers. Because most of such counseling is done in the local church, the counselor might be tempted to neglect and make assumptions about the spiritual condition of the counselee and move right to the counselee's problems. A primary principle in biblical counseling is not to assume anything, including whether the counselee is a true believer in Jesus Christ as Savior. To bypass the spiritual heart condition of the counselee is to be negligent as a counselor.

Counseling, Witnessing, and Discipleship

When believers understand what it means to be a believer, they are called to be witnesses of what Christ has done for them. It is suggested that the counselor not just look over a form filled out by the counselee where a short statement on personal salvation is written. As noted earlier, the beginning of a counseling session is a good time to ask counselees to verbally share how they became Christians. Having someone articulate his faith in Christ gives the counselor confidence that the counselee is a believer. Having the privilege of leading a counselee to faith in Christ is a part of biblical counseling which is very rewarding for the counselor. Biblical counseling also includes discipling others. Matthew 28:18b–20 states, *Jesus came to them* [disciples] *and said, All authority in heaven has been given to me. Therefore go* [or, as you are going] *and make disciples of all nations, baptizing them in the name of the Father and of the Son and of the Holy Spirit, and teaching them to obey everything I have commanded you. And surely, I will be with you always, to the very end of the age.*

Jesus had a pattern or plan when He called his disciples. First, He called them by name, which implies He knew them. Second, He asked them to join Him or to follow Him. Third, He shared His purpose, which was to make them fishers of men. In Acts 1:8 He told His disciples after His resurrection and before He ascended to heaven, *But you will receive power when the Holy Spirit comes on you; and you will be my witnesses in Jerusalem, and in all Judea and Samaria, and to the ends of the earth.* The counselor must adhere to this mandate in the context of counseling. Sharing Christ, leading an individual to personal faith in Christ, and discipling the counselee are the great privileges the counselor has. The counselor should never underestimate the power of the gospel in changing the human heart.

God's Gift: Grace

The last consideration for the counselor is to <u>always extend the gift of grace</u> in diagnosing the counselee's problem. If sin is part of the issue with the counselee, two attitudes will be projected, the first of which is an attitude of self-condemnation. This will be seen in bitterness, depression, defeatism, sinful lifestyle, anger, addiction, marital and family dysfunction, and so on. Such an attitude will be observed by the counselor during the counseling sessions. These attributes clearly reflect the thinking, attitude, and behavior of the counselee. Scripture that addresses self-condemning thoughts can be found in John 8:34 (NASB), *Truly, truly, I say to you, everyone who commits sin is the slave of sin* and Galatians 5:19–22 (NASB), *Now the deeds of the flesh are evident, which are: immorality, impurity, sensuality, idolatry, sorcery, enmities, strife, jealousy, outburst of anger, disputes, dissensions, factions, envying, drunkenness, carousing, and things like these, of which I forewarn you, just as I have forewarned you, that those who practice such things will not inherit the kingdom of God.*

The second is an attitude of self-exaltation. This attitude is characterized by a spirit of cover-up. The individual projects an air of pride reflected with a veneer of self-righteousness. The cover-up consists of a disguising behavior intended to convince others that everything is great. These individuals strive to be successful, and seek approval, recognition, and acceptance. However, they can also be judgmental, having a critical spirit, and be argumentative and divisive. Scriptural support to consider includes:

📖Proverbs 16:18 (NASB): *Pride goes before destruction and a haughty spirit before stumbling.*

📖Matthew 23:25, 26: *Woe to you, scribes and Pharisees, hypocrites! For you clean the outside of the cup and of the dish, but inside they are full of robbery and self-indulgence. You blind Pharisee! First clean the inside of the cup and of the dish, so that the outside of it may become clean also.*

When such attitudes are expressed, the counselor begins to share the antidote to such thinking, attitudes, and behaviors. The counselor should take the counselee through Scripture and explain the place of the grace of God through Jesus Christ who has offered forgiveness, grace and mercy for the believer. Hebrews 4:16: T*herefore let us draw near with confidence to the throne of grace, so that we may receive mercy and find grace to help in time of need.* 2 Peter 3:18: *But grow in the grace and knowledge of our Lord and Savior Jesus Christ. To him be glory both now and forever! Amen.* Once counselees understand the wonderful gift of grace on their behalf, they begin to change their attitudes and spirits to that of being thankful and grateful for all that God has done for them.

The gift of grace extended to the counselee is often a stumbling block. Counselees may conclude that they are unique, that God can't possibly forgive or accept them by offering His grace. Or they may conclude they aren't that bad in comparison to others.

All counselees must realize that it's not about them, but instead all about God. A few passages that underscore this change are

> Colossians 3:15 (NASB): *Let the peace of Christ rule in your hearts, to which indeed you were called in one body; and be thankful.*

> Colossians 2:6–7: *Therefore as you have received Christ Jesus the Lord, so walk in him, having been firmly rooted and now being built up in him and established in your faith, just as you were instructed, and overflowing with gratitude.*

The goal in the Christian life is to be conformed to the likeness of God's Son (see Romans 8:28–39). Once counselees recognize this goal for their own lives, there will be a freeing-up, a liberating motivation to live with the spirit and attitude of thanksgiving in all things. The counselor drives home these considerations and offers to the counselee the greatest message known to humanity: that of forgiveness and acceptance which provides the power to overcome and the grace of God that will transform one's life.

PART III

Protecting the Church

10

Legal Issues in Counseling

The church must take seriously the admonition about due diligence when it comes to setting up the counseling ministry lawfully. The passage in 1 Corinthians 14:33, *For God is not a God of disorder but of peace*, reminds us that everything should be done in a fitting and orderly way in the context of worship. However, it is incumbent upon the church to recognize the application of this passage as it relates to all aspects of the church's ministry, including the counseling ministry.

Whether the church is involved in counseling only church members or offering counseling as a ministry to the community, there are some legal guidelines to follow. The leadership team assigned to train members to counsel should cover all the bases when it comes to organizing the ministry. Romans 12:8 speaks to this issue: *If a man's gift is leadership, let him govern diligently.*

Before a local church begins a counseling ministry, the church must examine what the requirements and regulations are according to the state law. Each state's laws will vary for licensed counseling and pastoral counseling. However, there are certain laws recognized by all states with which the local church must comply.

All counselors and counselees must read and understand the church's philosophy and recognize the distinctive nature of biblical counseling. This document must be signed, dated, and kept by the church. Church counseling, according to state law, falls into the category of pastoral counseling and thus is distinguished from counseling undertaken by licensed counselors, psychologists, or

When I became counselor and director of the Biblical Counseling and Education Center under Calvary Bible College and Theological Seminary, I recognized the concern that we should do things decently and in order, which included a knowledge of the law in the state of Missouri. I contacted a local attorney to make sure we would not be in violation of the law and subject to litigation for malpractice. The law for Missouri (Mo. Rev. Stat. § 337.505 [1991]) reads, "State laws do not apply to: Duly ordained ministers or clergy or religious workers while functioning in their ministerial capacity." Bullis and Mazur (1993, p. 52) advise that "the First Amendment will protect clearly spiritual and religious counseling that is authorized by the denomination, sect, or religious body .... Additionally, these religious counselors should possess an accurate, current job description specifically detailing the amount of counseling and the type of counseling the position requires." Whether it is a counseling center or counseling in the local church, issues related to the law must become a priority.

psychiatrists. This dictates that the church must be consistent and stay within the boundaries of biblical (spiritual) counseling. I would encourage a church that is interested in establishing a counseling ministry to Google state requirements for pastoral counseling. Input the name of your state and it will give you all the information you need.

Whether the counselors are church staffers or lay members, it is important that as they counsel, they should never comment on or give a medical or psychological opinion to a counselee. When needed, it is advised that a counselor refer a counselee to a medical physician or any other professional in specific areas outside the boundaries of the biblical counselor. Not to do so leaves the church vulnerable and open to litigation. This warning must be given frequently throughout the training of counselors. The point is, do not beg for trouble. At all costs, avoid inferring, through statements and/or comments, anything other than the position of biblical counseling.

While serving as a pastor and training lay counselors, I was privileged to confide in two church members, a medical doctor and an attorney who had a biblical worldview, to assist me with their expertise from their professions. If a pastor does not have these types of professionals in the church, it would be to his advantage to get acquainted with Christian professionals in his community.

The following guidelines will assist the church in getting her house in order according to the laws of the state as they relate to pastoral counseling.

Legal Policies and Forms

The local church must add a malpractice insurance policy, which is usually available as an inexpensive rider to the church's existing insurance policy. This policy covers counseling activities, as well as other activities of the church that may be related to the counseling program.

All individuals being recruited to serve as counselors must fill out an Application for Counseling form (see Appendix D), accompanied with a screening and criminal background check that is signed, dated, and kept by the church and renewed annually. This includes those working with children as well as those serving as counselors. The counselors who have been approved by the church leadership must read and understand the church's philosophy and the distinctive nature and attributes of biblical counseling. This church statement is to be signed, dated, and filed as well.

A question is often asked concerning what must be reported by law in the counseling ministry. Is the church exempt from such reporting? These are good questions, and the answer is that all counselors must adhere to the limits of confidentiality (see Appendix E), under the following circumstances:

- When a counselee intends to take harmful, dangerous, or criminal action against himself or another individual

- When a client or the client's family is likely to suffer threats of or the results of harmful behavior

- Where there is a reasonable suspicion of the abuse of elderly persons or children under the age of 18.

In these circumstances, the church is not exempt and under the law must report such occurrences.

A Permission to Consult or consent release form (see Appendix F) signed by the counselee must be filed and kept confidentially at the church. This form gives the counselor permission to contact any individual outside the counseling session. Maliska addressed the parameters for referral: "Biblical counseling may need, on rare occasion, an appropriate referral service. Example of the types of cases that would be referred may include the following: medically related problems, suspected medical problems, prescription drug regulation and consultation, court cases requiring testing and reporting from a licensed psychiatrist or psychologist, and dangerous behavior that may require supervision to preserve the life of a counselee and those around him/her" (1988).

It would be good practice for the counseling program to include a Minor Consent of Minor form (see Appendix G) for all counseling with those under the age of 18. This form should be signed, dated, and kept confidentially at the church counseling office. Because most church counselors are not state licensed, it is advised that volunteer counselors should not counsel minors. There are churches that will counsel minors as long as the parents are present.

The counseling office should keep all counseling files, forms, and other counseling-related items in secure, locked filing cabinets. Keys to the cabinets must be kept by and available to authorized personnel only. It is suggested that the locked filing cabinets be kept in a designated room out of sight from the public.

The Brotherhood Mutual Insurance Company publication, *The Deacon's Bench* (1995), presents a serious warning to the church about the risk of sexual misconduct, which tops the list of causes for pastoral counseling lawsuits. A few rules should be in place to avoid undue temptation. For example, counseling should be done at the church in a designated counseling room. The interior door to the room should have a window, to avoid any appearance of inappropriate behavior. Additionally, the church should consider where the counseling office and counseling rooms should be located. This would be helpful for counselees who are unacquainted with the church building. Easy access from the outside must be considered and clear directions to the counseling office posted. For convenience, restrooms and a water fountain should be located nearby.

The church may seek legal guidance from organizations such as The Christian Law Association (www.christianlaw.org), which produces a monthly publication called *Legal Alert*. This publication presents up-to-date articles on laws and their application to and impact on the church. Along with that publication, the CLA provides free legal services paid for in part from the generosity of God's people. The CLA has been serving Bible-believing churches and Christians since 1969.

The church may investigate what organizations are available locally that provide legal advocacy based on biblical standards of justice. Such organizations provide a referral network of Christian lawyers to satisfy most legal needs.

I cannot stress enough the importance of knowing and complying with state laws and regulations in counseling for the local church. We live in a litigious society, and if the church is naïve regarding the requirements for counseling in the church, God forbid, the church could face a very damaging lawsuit. Keep in mind that a church can address all the issues discussed in this chapter and still face litigation. However, having proper documentation and forms will certainly be an advantage during such a time. Do your homework and cover your bases before ever considering launching a counseling ministry. Steve Levicoff, in his book *Christian Counseling and the Law*, wisely wrote, "Your best protection as a counselor is not to hold yourself out to be more than you're qualified to be. If you are a trained lay Christian counselor, you should not be purporting to be a professional counselor. If you are a pastor, your business cards should not refer to you as a 'professional counselor.' The fact that counseling will be a significant part of your pastoral ministry is a given assumption. But your counseling should be in the pastoral context and should not imply credentials that you may not have" (1991, p. 47).

Once the church has knowledge of the requirements, regulations, and laws, it must incorporate them as policies of the church's counseling ministry. All policies must be printed, read, and signed by the counselees who come in for counseling services. The church must guard against overlooking any loopholes that could put the church in jeopardy.

As the counseling ministry grows, the church may consider an outreach to the community. The next chapter, chapter 11, investigates models to be considered in establishing a broader counseling scope.

11

Counseling Models in the
Church and Community

For just as each of us has one body with many members, and these members do not all have the same function, so in Christ we who are many form one body, and each member belongs to all the others.
Romans 12:4, 5

Having an effective counseling ministry, in both the church and the community, requires proper administration and organization by the leadership. As noted in chapter 10, much has to be considered regarding policies, forms, documentation, knowledge of state laws, and the like. If the church is not willing to do its homework in these matters, it should not consider establishing a counseling ministry. Reaching out to the community with counseling services demands that the church plan for and meet all legal requirements. The church should consider the wise counsel from Proverbs 15:22, 16:3: *Plans fail for lack of counsel, but with many advisors they succeed. Commit to the Lord whatever you do, and your plans will succeed.*

The following overview of counseling models may be used to help the church establish a counseling ministry in the church and community.

The Local Church Model

The local church model, as the name indicates, is set up within the framework of the local church. The advantage of this model is that it uses the pastoral staff and volunteer counselors within the church. The church uses a rider on the church insurance policy for counseling liability to cover all counselors. Under this model, the accountability for the counseling program lies with the ruling board of the church. The budget for the program is part of the overall church budget. The counseling budget should indicate itemized expenses, such as advertising and promotional materials, counseling materials and resources, professional training, secretarial assistance, and so on. Facilities for counseling offices, and provision for refreshments and supplies, are to be provided by the church and reflected in the budget. All policies are set by the church and the counseling staff adheres to the organizational structure and procedures. It is suggested that such policies be incorporated into the bylaws of the church constitution as well as a manual for all who counsel in the program. The church may consider a committee or board designated to oversee the counseling ministry of the church.

Full-Time Church Counselor

This model is set up very similarly to the local church model. The difference is that the counselor is hired full time and oversees the counseling ministry. This position might be titled Counseling Director, and the person in this position would be a member of the pastoral staff. This individual should be experienced in counseling, well trained, and usually have a degree in biblical counseling (preferably a master's degree or greater). It also would be appropriate for the counselor/director to be certified with recognized biblical counseling agencies (see Appendix B). It is the responsibility of the church to develop a job description for this position that includes objectives, requirements, responsibilities, authority, accountability, work tasks, standard of performance, and evaluation.

There are multiple objectives for a person in this position:

1. To be responsible for the development and promotion of the counseling program.

2. To train church members, leadership, and others involved in the counseling ministry.

3. To provide counseling materials and resources for both.

4. To give oversight for all counselors and counselees.

5. To be the point person overseeing all aspects of the counseling ministry of the church.

Requirements and responsibilities for the full-time counselor include promotion of the counseling ministry within the membership of the church, as well as in outreach to the community. Secondly, this individual supervises the operational aspects of the counseling ministry, and thirdly becomes the director and primary counselor in the church. As the director, this person is responsible for developing a yearly budget for the counseling ministry and keeping proper financial records. The director also needs to identify and solicit professional referrals with a biblical worldview and biblical counseling philosophy. Other responsibilities for this position include developing prayer support for the ministry; reporting directly to the pastoral/leadership board regarding the development of the counseling ministry; and developing, providing, and preparing effective materials and resources to be used in promoting the ministry through the church and community outreach. Lastly, the director must meet the ethical and professional standards set by biblical counseling certification agencies.

Community Counseling Center

A counseling center serves the community by providing a place to which many churches in the community can refer their people for counseling. The purpose of the counseling ministry is to make available to the community biblical insights and answers regarding life's challenges and dilemmas. Pastors in the community with similar faith and theology can come together and support a counseling center with qualified and certified biblical counselors working full or part time to meet the needs of the churches in the community. This type of arrangement, often set up by several small churches, takes the counseling load off any single church yet provides confidence in the counseling center, because of the center staff's sharing a philosophy and biblical methodology.

This model has a broader geographical outreach. Through referrals by churches, parachurch ministries, and other organizations, the center can meet many needs in the community. As the center becomes established, it will begin to grow through word of mouth by those who have received help in their lives.

> Our college and seminary had a radio station where my wife and I conducted a 15-minute daily counseling program. After the program was aired, the phone at the counseling center became very active with people calling to schedule a time for counseling.

Qualified Counselors

The counselors serving at the center should be experienced, educationally trained in counseling, and professionally certified through a respectable biblical counseling agency. The educational training and certification ensure more knowledgeable and credible staff members who can deal with behavioral issues and a wide range of counseling problems, which instills confidence for the counselees. As a center, the staff is focused on counseling and is available to work consistently with a counselee without disruptions, as opposed to counseling by a pastor who has many other church responsibilities and probably very little available time.

Counseling Services

The staff of the center can provide counseling seminars, training, and other related services for churches and other community organizations. It is a great advantage for the community to have such a ministry, that is sponsored by churches and Christian organizations, with biblical counseling opportunities. This is especially true in smaller communities that may not have the same counseling opportunities as bigger market areas.

Church Connections

As a referral agency, the biblical counseling center is unique in that it works in concert with the local church, not apart from it. If counselees are referred by a church, they are required to meet with a church leader weekly to communicate what they are learning and how they are progressing in personal spiritual growth. Each counselee is encouraged to communicate to a church pastor all that he or she is learning at the center. This procedure keeps the pastor abreast of how the counselee is benefiting spiritually from the counseling while dealing with personal problems. This process develops a reciprocal effect whereby the pastor is encouraged by the counselee's progress and he can keep encouraging the counselee to continue with the counseling. If the pastor needs clarity from the counselor, with the counselee's permission, he could talk to or meet with the counselor. This arrangement can also assist the counselor in providing the best level of care. The pastor knows the counselee, so his knowledge and insights would be very valuable for the counselor.

This is a win/win situation, as both the counselor and the pastor want to see counselees grow in the Lord, and have a biblical change in their thinking, attitudes, and behaviors. This is especially beneficial to a pastor when he finds himself trying to deal with members of his church who present difficult problems that he just doesn't have time or the expertise to deal with. Therefore, the pastor can be selective with his own involvement in counseling for short-term issues, but has a referral option to the counseling center staff when a long-term, difficult situation arises.

Such a counseling center is well equipped, with proper materials, forms, policies, homework material (growth projects), and resources, to give counselees maximum exposure and assistance in meeting their needs. This model provides for good recordkeeping and proper files, which are kept confidential throughout the counseling process. This type of center also usually has a hotline that individuals can call during working hours for prayer and assistance in dealing with emergency issues. In situations where a counselee is in crisis beyond the scope of what the center can handle, the counselor networks with related agencies to refer emergency cases to community mental health, social, and professional services.

The Counseling Center Receptionist

The receptionist at the center handles all calls for scheduling and addressing questions. This person is responsible for mailing materials (policies, appointments, procedures, etc.) to counselees. The secretary/receptionist keeps all files in order, keeps the office clean and presentable, orders supplies and materials, and keeps a good supply of refreshments on hand. Often counselees need to reschedule their appointments, and the receptionist must coordinate all scheduling and rescheduling with the counselors. Without a competent person in this position, the counseling center tends to be chaotic and can lose its credibility and effectiveness. A well-organized counseling center, fully supplied and functioning professionally, instills confidence in the churches and individuals that use the counseling services.

The Counseling Center Director

The director of the counseling center serves as the overseer and promoter of the ministry. This person develops the budget, raises funds, develops policies, and works with the board of the center. The board could be formed of members of supporting churches, organizations, and business individuals (those of like faith and in agreement with the counseling philosophy).

Organizationally, a counseling center may serve as an extension ministry of a church, a parachurch ministry, or a Christian college/ seminary. Being affiliated with one of these types of ministries signals to the community that the center is not a fly-by-night operation. If it is an extension of a church, however, it must be communicated to the community that the position of the church is not to proselytize or set demands on individuals regarding church involvement. Nevertheless, the help that the counselee receives may be motivation to attend one of the supporting churches.

Financial Arrangements

Counseling centers normally set fees for counseling services. In some cases, churches that refer members to the center may invest in the counseling of their members by covering the fee or a portion of it. A center may consider adjusting the fee for those who can't afford counseling, and perhaps solicit funds from the community to underwrite such efforts. A heavy financial burden for the center is the salaries for the counselors. Similar to missionaries, the counselors may raise all or part of their support through committed donors. Fundraising events in the community may cover expenditures by the center, or at least help in this area. Churches, Christian organizations, and community agencies may provide funds from their budgets to support this valuable ministry. The board of the counseling center should include an ongoing role to promote and fundraise for the financial needs of the center.

Satellite Centers

As the former director of the counseling center in Kansas City, Missouri (Calvary), the author recognized a need to branch out to serve the metropolitan area. The main center was on the school's campus on the south side of Kansas City. As the need for the center grew, three other satellite centers (north, east, and west) were established and provided closer, more convenient sites for people to access a biblical counseling center. Calls for counseling were received through the main center, and that secretary set up the appointments between counselor and counselee. The secretary also sent out material that included directions to the satellite location, along with other material to be filled out and taken to the counselor. Of the three centers, two were located in churches and one was in a Christian ministry facility. The counselors were seminary students who were majoring in biblical counseling and in their last year were fulfilling their counseling project requirements. Each student was under my authority and supervision, since I was the chair of the biblical counseling program as well as the director of the counseling centers. All counselees were told that they would be meeting with students from the seminary as part of their program requirements. If the counselees were uncomfortable with student counselors, they were encouraged to attend the main counseling center where I was the counselor. Most counselees were fine with meeting with students under those conditions.

Counseling Facilities

Facilities for our counseling centers were provided without charge by the two churches, and the third satellite center was sponsored by a Christian organization. A contract for use of the facility was developed for each satellite site. This was a basic signed agreement between the main counseling center and the host facility. The contract described responsibilities for both the counseling center and the host facility. For example, the host facility responsibilities might be to provide an office to be used by the counseling center on Monday and Wednesday mornings (9:00 a.m. to 12:00 noon) and Tuesday and Thursday evenings (6:00 p.m. to 9:00 p.m.). Any additional times had to be cleared, in advance, with the church/

facility administrator. The facility provided liability insurance coverage for the counselor and counselee while on the property. (Note: In some cases, insurance provision may be covered by the main center.) The facility was to provide a file cabinet that could be locked and accessed only by the counseling center personnel. The counseling center agreed to provide a counselor and to schedule counseling sessions at the facility at designated times. Counseling fees were processed through the center, with monthly reports given to the church regarding the number of counseling cases and use of the facilities. All appointments and finances were coordinated from the main counseling center by the secretary/receptionist. Counseling training or seminars were scheduled to be given at the supporting agencies whose facilities were used, to show appreciation for the partnership.

In this model, the director of the primary counseling center oversees all counselors and is responsible for the administration of the satellite centers. The counseling staff are accountable to the director and attend monthly meetings to discuss counseling issues and other related topics. The director oversees the budget, monitors all counseling sessions, and represents the counseling ministry.

This model is unique in that the overhead costs are kept to a minimum because there is no cost for facilities, materials, supplies, and the like. The counselors received a portion of the counseling fee, along with academic credit in the counseling program. All counselees understood that the counseling fee was discounted because the counselor was still a student. The director supervised and monitored all students participating as counselors.

Benefits of Student Counselors

Student counselors provide benefits for both the institution and the community. The institution provides the student with needed counseling experience. It also helps the student to meet the counseling practicum and internship requirements of the seminary program. For the community and churches, the benefits came from the opportunity to offer biblical counseling in their geographical area with reasonable counseling fees. The community recognized that through the partnership with the institution, it enabled students to receive valuable experience as counselors.

Finally, in this model, if a student struggled in counseling a counselee about an issue the student felt personally inadequate to deal with, the supervisor either stepped in and team-counseled with the student, or a more experienced counselor was provided to work with the counselee. This arrangement is another example of how this model is mutually beneficial for the people seeking counseling, the community, and the institution.

Outreach in Multiple Cities

A multiple-city outreach model is a unique model in which a church/center utilizes a full-time counselor assigned to cover a territory serving nearby areas. The church provides a salary for the counselor, but revenue is supplemented by the cities/towns the counselor serves. Monies may come from counseling fees, church budgets, or donations by those who believe in the ministry.

The participating cities can have a counselor in their town one or two days a week, or whatever is negotiated for the need in that city. Promotion is through churches, organizations, radio, and newspapers in each town. Facilities are provided at no charge and counselees pay a fee for the counseling. Business offices can also be provided for this service. Elements from each model should apply regarding staff, insurance, files, materials, supplies, training, and budgets.

This chapter has presented models available to assist the local church in biblical counseling. Each model is unique, and so may not be appropriate for a given location. There are specific models that would work best for small towns with small churches; in cities with megachurches and parachurch ministries, one of the other models may just be what would meet their needs. Regardless of the size of a town, biblical counseling is a valuable resource for the community which can be implemented through one of the various models. When a pastor feels unprepared to counsel or does not have interest or time for an ongoing counseling ministry (due to sermon preparation, studying, praying, visitation, administration, board and committee meetings, family and marital responsibilities, etc.), a counseling model would be a welcomed ministry.

Ministries Available Through Biblical Counseling

Students studying biblical counseling have many opportunities to serve the local community as they prepare for ministry after graduation. For example, biblical counselors may serve as pastors, youth workers, chaplains (hospital, military, nursing homes, fire/police, Christian medical clinics, professional athletic organizations, etc.); in post-abortion and preventative abortion clinics and/or rescue missions; as counselors in Christian schools; as Christian camp counselors; in Christian radio ministry; and as counselors in mission agencies. Our seminary's program of offering students experience in counseling while earning their degrees is unique in the academic world. This model gives students a jump-start in developing their skill in counseling, which prepares them for ministry. This model is another innovative approach for counseling in the community.

12

The Counselor as a Peacemaker

Whatever you have learned or received or heard from me, or seen in me—put it into practice. And the God of peace will be with you.
Philemon 4:9

When a counselor meets with a counselee, the problems have escalated and the counselee is out of options; as a last measure, such a person turns to a counselor. The counselor might as well realize that this is a given in the counseling arena. The counselor must meet counselees where they are, with all the attendant mess, emotional distress, conflict, and crisis. Adding to this, the counselee may not desire to be in counseling.

As previously stated in this book, a counselor has several roles depending on the circumstances. These roles may include serving as a coach, teacher, or mentor, or possibly being involved in discipling. In addition, the counselor may also need to serve as a peacemaker.

James 3:17, 18 (NASB) reads, *But the wisdom from above is first pure, then peaceable, gentle, reasonable, full of mercy and good fruits, unwavering, without hypocrisy. And the seed whose fruit is righteousness is sown in peace by those who make peace.* The biblical word for "peace" carries the meaning of a quiet and gentle manner with the aim of reconciling quarrels and being oneself in peace with all men. In Matthew 5:1–12, Jesus gives the beatitudes from the Sermon on the Mount. In verse 9, He says, *Blessed are the peacemakers, for they shall see God.* In James 3:17, 18, this same word for "peacemaker" is used again: *But the wisdom that comes from heaven is first of all pure; then peace loving, considerate, submissive, full of mercy and good fruit, impartial and sincere. Peacemakers who sow in peace raise a harvest of righteousness.* James further develops this theme in chapter 4:1–4 and gives an answer as to why there is so much conflict. He asks, *What causes fights and quarrels among you? Don't they come from your desires that battle within you? You want something but don't get it. You kill and covet, but you cannot have what you want. You quarrel and fight. You do not have, because you do not ask God. When you ask, you do not receive, because you ask with wrong motives, that you may spend what you get on your pleasures.* In verses 1 and 2, lusts are described as pleasures to crave after, to desire, to seek one's own will instead of God's. There is a spirit of discord with fights and quarrels among you. The discord comes from wanting to satisfy oneself without considering the other party. "You want something but don't get it." This is due to the desire to satisfy oneself only. It is within reach but not actually received. James continues in verse 2 by saying, *You do not have, because you do not ask.* In other words, the answer to your problem is to pray to God, but James acknowledges there is prayerlessness instead. Lastly, in verse 3 James describes a wrongful or sinful act of praying with wrong motives. The solution to such a condition is given in verse 6: *But He gives us more grace.* Therefore, the solution is God's grace. He giveth is in the present tense, indicating that God gives habitually. Humans are the recipients of God's grace and our response is not out of pride but through humility. Therefore, verse 6 continues by stating: *God opposes the proud but gives grace to the humble.*

As previously mentioned, a large percentage of counseling consists of dealing with conflict and crisis in the life of the counselee. These situations create challenges that affect one's emotional, spiritual, mental, social, and relational areas of life. Panic, confusion, and fear set in. Decision making becomes distorted, relationships become strained, and motivation is stymied. Escape attempts take the form of shutting down emotionally, displaying outbursts of anger, turning to substance abuse, conducting extramarital affairs, and running away both physically and emotionally. Other behaviors springing from conflict and crisis are displayed as spiritual confusion, doubting God, questioning one's salvation, having weak faith, and withdrawing from church life, family members, and others. Persons in such states of crisis often cease reading the Bible or praying. A self-pitying attitude — a "why me?" mentality — appears the longer the crisis continues. These persons consider their crisis or conflict to be unique from any others. This is why counselees often claim that the counselor can't relate to or understand their situation because the counselor hasn't personally been through such experiences.

Criticism of Biblical Counseling

Counselors have their work cut out for them when dealing with those going through conflict. Does the Bible address such matters? After all, this is the twenty-first century and the Bible is old and archaic. What approach should a counselor take in dealing with such difficult issues? Should the counselor refer the counselee to a more professional counselor, concluding that any biblical counseling methodology is inadequate? These questions deserve answers.

It should be noted that some church counselors might in fact be inadequate to deal with some types of matters. However, this has nothing to do with a falsely perceived inadequacy or irrelevance of the Bible. Instead, it is due to a lack of knowledge and experience on the part of the counselor. It is at this point that counselors must be honest and admit their limitations in counseling. In this situation, a need for more training, and further studying and researching of the Bible, are needed. Counseling is demanding and humbling and should not be attempted by the novice in faith or in counseling practice. This is true in other careers as well. For instance, not all car mechanics can diagnose every problem and repair every car accurately. Doctors can be baffled by a patient's condition. In these instances, professionals look to others for a second opinion. The point is this: the car manual by the manufacturer or the medical books are not the issue. The issue is the mechanic and the doctor. Their pride may not allow them to admit their limitations, or their genuine humility may recognize that others with greater knowledge and experience should be consulted.

This chapter attempts to assist the lay counselor in dealing biblically with crisis/conflict counseling. How does a counselor work through the maze of elements affecting a counselee? What guidance by the counselor can be helpful in understanding a crisis and dealing with conflict?

In the Chinese language, the word "crisis" is composed of the characters for two other words: "danger" and "opportunity." Opportunity implies the idea of growth and maturation as one goes through a crisis. The counselee needs to realize that God is there during any crisis and to recognize the opportunities that may come from the crisis. Ephesians 5:15–17 says, *Be very careful, then, how to live—not as unwise but as wise, making the most of every opportunity, because the days are evil. Therefore, do not be foolish, but understand what the Lord's will is.*

Danger appears in the crisis when one ignores the resources available to deal with the crisis. Psalm 91:1, 2, 14–16 is a fitting passage for the believer in a crisis:

> *He who dwells in the shelter of the Most High will rest in the shadow of the Almighty. I will say to the Lord, "He is my refuge and my fortress, my God, in whom I trust." Because he loves me, says the Lord, I will rescue him; I will protect him, for he acknowledges my name. He will call upon me, and I will answer*

him; I will be with him in trouble, I will deliver him and honor him. With life will I satisfy him and show him my salvation.

Biblical Premise

The believer has the power of the Holy Spirit to overcome inherent difficulties that humankind faces, and the Bible gives guidance as a foundation for dealing with life difficulties. In biblical counseling, the counselor is personal, caring, and a brother or sister in the Lord. The counseling approach is not based on theory, nor on the counselor's opinion concerning life issues. The biblical counselor does not guide counselees to look within themselves and decide what is the right decision they should make by what they feel is right. The counselor's approach is to develop a biblical worldview and help counselees ground their decisions on the clear principles and commands found in the Bible.

In Psalm 19:7–10, David proclaims, *The law of the Lord is perfect, reviving the soul.* This indicates that the law is complete and sufficient. "Reviving" carries the meaning "to restore" or "to transform." *The statutes of the Lord are trustworthy, making wise the simple* (v. 7). This is a great encouragement that the Word can be fully trusted, and that thereby one can have confidence, knowing that its application will work. This gives the counselee guidance in making the right choices in life. *The precepts of the Lord are right, giving joy to the heart* (v. 8). There is no confusion for the counselee. The Word is clear and accurate, giving proper direction to follow. Following the Word for one's life has an inner, emotional outcome. *The commands of the Lord are radiant, giving light to the eyes* (v. 8b). The Word illuminates one's thinking and insight. Psalm 119:37 reads, *Turn my eyes away from worthless things; renew my life according to your Word.* In the same chapter, verse 18 states, *Open my eyes that I may see wonderful things in your law.* Verse 24 says, *Your statutes are my delight; they are my counselors.*

Psalm 19:9 continues, *The fear of the Lord is pure, enduring forever. The ordinances of the Lord are sure and altogether righteous.* The Word is flawless and relevant; it has long-term, eternal effects. The counsel of the Word does not have to be questioned. It is unadulterated truth. *They are more precious than gold, than much pure gold; they are sweeter than honey, than honey from the comb* (v. 10). Notice that the law, statutes, precepts, commands, fear, and ordinances are all in the context of the Lord. Therefore, the counselee can be assured that the authority and sufficiency of the Scriptures are the platform for biblical counseling. This is genuine hope, not "hope so" or blind hope, but hope based on the testimony of the Lord and His Word. The goal is to bring about change that brings glory to God. The Christian counselor relies on change that comes from within by the supernatural work of God to bring healing to the soul, through repentance, forgiveness, reconciliation, and restoration between God and humans. This kind of change brings about transformation that will be long term as a person is obedient to the Scriptures.

The context of dealing with conflict is found in the local church. In The Peacemaker (2005, p. 14), Sande writes, "The Lord has provided a powerful support system for peacemaking. It is the church. When we are unable to resolve a conflict on our own God commands the local church to step in and bring its wisdom, resources, and authority to bear on the problem. (Matt. 18:16–17; Phil. 4:2–3; I Cor. 6:1–8) Churches are teaching their people to be peacemakers, training gifted members to serve as conflict coaches and mediators, and reinstating the ministry of loving, redemptive accountability to restore members who have become entangled in destructive sin."

Biblical Counselor Is a Peacemaker

There's a tongue-in-cheek saying that where two or three are gathered together, there will be conflict. There's a certain amount of truth in this statement. A similar statement goes this way: "To dwell above with those we love, oh, that will be glory. To dwell below with those we know, well, that's another story." Many can relate to and identify with such sentiments. Those in ministry know that it is not a bed of roses by any means. Ministers rarely leave a church due to doctrinal differences; rather, they leave because they lack "people skills" and are unable to deal with conflict. Seminaries would do well to add a course in conflict resolution, to help prepare the pastoral student to face conflict in the church. Once the student begins his ministry, he soon encounters church members who are riddled with crisis and conflict and are searching for help and clear guidance from the pastor. Therefore, a biblical training program is a must for equipping the counselor in conflict/crisis counseling.

The Scriptures, from Genesis to Revelation, give the counselor much material related to dealing with conflict. Biblical words that express conflict and crisis include *strife, disputes, quarrels, contention (quarrelsome), dissention (disagreements)*, and *discord*. Conflict abounds in the lives of biblical characters such as Moses, Abraham, Joseph, David, Jonah, Job, Philemon, Joseph, and Mary, as well as the disciples and apostles. In studying these individuals, along with the various churches in the New Testament, it becomes evident that conflict/crisis is found in almost every book of the Bible. A study of the life and teachings of Christ alone yields an exorbitant amount of material. One concludes, by studying these examples, that conflict touches all aspects of life: personal, interpersonal, family, business/career, racial, gender, religious belief and values, and much more.

Peacemaking

Jesus announced to his disciples, in John 14:27: *Peace I leave with you; my peace I give you. I do not give to you as the world gives. Do not let your heart be troubled and do not be afraid.* The counselee needs to realize that God is there during any crisis and to recognize the opportunities that may come from the crisis. The phrase *The Lord is peace* comes from the name of God Himself, Jehovah Shalom (Judges 6:11–23). This passage informs us that Gideon was hiding, in mortal danger. When God appeared as an angel and assured him that all would be well, he declared, *The Lord is peace* (Jehovah Shalom). Judges 6:24 announces: *Then Gideon built an altar and named it, the Lord of peace.*

The Apostle Paul wrote to the church at Philippi: *Do not be anxious about anything, but in everything, by prayer and petition, with thanksgiving, present your requests to God. And the peace of God, which transcends all understanding, will guard your hearts and your minds in Christ Jesus* (Philemon 4:6, 7). It has been said that to know the peace of God, one must know the God of peace.

The Lord desires that the believer trust Him in everything. This includes everything from huge commitments to the very smallest details. Jesus is asking the believer to trust that He will keep our lives together in a way that brings honor to Him. This book mentions the T.A.B. approach many times. It all starts with thinking, followed by attitude and then behavior. Paul gives the challenge in Philippians 4:8: *Finally, brothers, whatever is true, whatever is noble, whatever is right, whatever is pure, whatever is lovely, whatever is admirable — if anything is excellent or praiseworthy — think about such things.* This is the antidote to fear, confusion, lack of trust, and struggles with one's faith. Sande (2005, p. 42) clearly explains this:

> When you are involved in a conflict, you too must decide whether you will trust God. Trusting God does not mean believing that he will do all that you want, but rather believing that he will do everything he knows is good. If you do not trust God, you will inevitably place your trust in yourself or another person, which ultimately leads to grief. On the other hand, if you believe that God is sovereign and that he will never allow

anything into your life unless it can be used for good, you will see conflicts not as accidents but as opportunities. This kind of trust glorifies God and inspires the faithfulness needed for effective peacemaking.

A familiar verse in the book of Romans 8:28 reads: *And we know that in all things God works for the good of those who love him, who have been called according to his purpose.* Notice that it does not tell us how God will work out all things; that is where trust on the believer's part is required. Secondly, the condition in which *all things work for the good* applies to those who love Him. 1 Corinthians 13 is known as the love chapter. In verse 7, Paul writes: *Love always protects, always trusts, always hopes, always perseveres.* If the counselee faces conflict with the prerequisite to love, which is an active verb, the fruit of that love will be demonstrated in trusting the Lord.

When the world seems to be a storm all around a counselee, it is then that the need is to turn to the One who calms the storms. The counselor encourages counselees not to wait until the last minute, when the circumstances of life are about to drown them, but to truly turn to Christ and trust Him.

Restoring Relationships
A counselor is to facilitate in bringing the counselee to restore relationships damaged due to conflict, just as Christ's death on the cross reconciled us to God. 2 Corinthians 5:17–18 (NASB) speaks to this issue: *Therefore, if anyone is in Christ, he is a new creature; the old things passed away; behold, new things have come. Now all these things are from God, who reconciled us to Himself through Christ and gave us the ministry of reconciliation.*

Reconciliation is to be between Christians as well. We have been brought into harmony with God, and by that reality we are brought into harmony with one another. When this harmony is broken, the relationship must be restored. This is not an option, but a command.

Galatians 6:1 describes the restoration process: *Brothers, if someone is caught in a sin, you who are spiritual should restore him gently.* Romans 15:1–2 also gives guidance in relationships: *We who are strong ought to bear with the failings of the weak and not to please ourselves. Each of us should please his neighbor for his good, to build him up.*

Many crises in life may create conflict with others, such as losing a job, the death of a loved one, an accident, financial difficulties, sickness/disease, and abusive situations, as well as many other situations. The conflict needs to be resolved, and the parties involved reconciled and restored with forgiveness extended to another.

When people have been hurt due to an upsetting experience, they often find it emotionally and mentally difficult to focus away from what has happened and look forward for quicker healing from the Lord.

Counselees often focus on the scars left from hurtful experiences, which will deter the healing process. They will talk to others

I recall when our daughter was young; she was playing outside with other children and suddenly ran into the house crying. She had fallen and scraped her knee; my wife consoled her, cleaned her knee, and put medicine and a bandage on it. My wife reassured her that it would heal and encouraged her to go back outside and play. My wife watched her as she joined her playmates. Then my wife observed our daughter doing something unexpected. She would go to her playmates and ask them if they wanted to see her "owie." She would take the Band Aid off and show them. I've reflected on that story many times as it relates to counseling and forgiveness.

about their hurtful condition over and over. They can't get past the one who offended them and look to the healer who *heals the brokenhearted and binds up their wounds* (Psalm 147:3). A Scriptural promise about the believer's future is in Revelation 21:4: *He will wipe every tear from their eyes. There will be no more death or mourning or crying or pain, for the old order of things has passed away.*

Personal Illustration of Restoration and Forgiveness
A lady who came to me for counseling had a strange request. She said she grew up in a dysfunctional, non-Christian home in which her mother was very mean to her and her other siblings. Her request was to pray to God and express from her heart that she forgave her mother for all the past sins against her. I inquired as to why she was doing this in my presence. Her answer was that she wanted me to be a witness that she had forgiven her mother. So, she prayed the prayer and looked at me and said that she felt better and thanked me for hearing her prayer.

I told her that was a big first step for her. She said, "A first step?" I replied that the second step was to go directly to her mother and ask for her forgiveness over the bitterness and resentment this lady had built up over the years. "Oh, I don't think I could do that, you don't know my mother," she exclaimed. I told her to go home and pray about it and when she felt that she should do that to come back. Several weeks went by before she finally came back. "You were right," she said, "and I need you to pray for me because I'm unsure how it will go in doing this with my mother." Of course, I was pleased to pray for her. She came back and thanked me for praying and shared that the visit with her mother had gone well. She stated that even though her mother denied having mistreated her, she nonetheless accepted the daughter's forgiveness for harboring ill feelings over the years toward her. I told this lady that she had taken ownership of her responsibility toward her mother, which is what God requires of her.

Then I told her she was now ready for step three. With a look of puzzlement, she asked what I meant by step three. I informed her that in our first session she indicated that she had spoken to her husband and children disrespectfully regarding her upbringing by her mean, unloving mother. "You need to gather your family together and ask for their forgiveness for your anger and disrespect you've communicated to them over the years towards your mother," I said. At that, she recognized her sin in her speech to her family and acknowledged to me that she must do that.

She came back for the third time and informed me how well it had gone when apologizing to her children and husband. She acknowledged the mean spirit she had had for years against her mother. She then said, "I sure hope there isn't another step I need to do." I said, "Well, there is one more step." She replied, "Really! What could that be?" I reminded her that she had told me that the only other Christian sibling in the family was one of her sisters. They lived miles apart but would frequently talk on the phone and often degrade and condemn their mother and the rest of the family members who were sinful. I communicated that she needed to call her sister and seek forgiveness. I noted that in all the years she had conversed with her sister, she had never prayed for her mother and family members nor discussed how they might model the Christian life before them. "Wow," she said. "Coming to you is brutal. You are so right, however, and I will call my sister this week and seek her forgiveness as well."

Once again, she came to see me. "Again," she said, "I followed through with the call to my sister and together over the phone we cried and prayed and forgave one another." I said, "Praise the Lord; I'm so proud of you in being obedient and doing the right thing. There is now harmony in your family, with your sister and mother. And I can't think of another step for you to take!" We both laughed and rejoiced together. I conclude this chapter with a prayer from 1 Peter 5:10: *And the God of all grace, who called you to his eternal glory in Christ, after you have suffered a little while, will restore you and make you strong, firm and steadfast.*

As mentioned earlier, counseling is painful, as people must address the conflict that has to be overcome in their lives. As Romans 12:17, 18 admonishes: *Do not repay anyone evil for evil. Be careful to do what is right in the eyes of everybody. If it is possible, as far as it depends on you live at peace with everyone.* For the counselor, the benefits far outweigh the liabilities. To see people break through to victory in which relationships are mended and reestablished is a blessing unsurpassed.

13

When All Else Fails: Church Discipline

A counseling program will be a great preventer to keep people from failing in relationships, crises, and major issues of life. Unfortunately, for many, counseling is considered a last-ditch effort after all other options have failed. The counselor faces this dilemma constantly, as people turn to counseling with very little hope that anything will change. This is the typical mindset when people come for counseling, so counselors have their work cut out for them to seek a biblical resolution and resolve that will lead to a proper change.

The counselor always prays that the counselee will be responsive to God's leading. There are wonderful testimonials by people who were very discouraged and ready to give up, only to see God work in their lives in a supernatural way. Not all testimonials end in such a "praise God" way, however. There are times when people harden their hearts, will not listen, and eventually walk out on counseling and never return. They turn their back on counseling from the Word of God, their church, family, and friends. There is nothing left but an ash heap of damaged relationships and failed efforts.

The counselor should never give up. God has a way of getting the attention of a counselee. Continue to pray even if counseling has ceased and pray that the counselee will eventually look to the Lord.

What often happens in the lives of counselees is that an attitude of sinful thinking and behavior has been such a part of life that it is hard to admit their wrongdoing. They tend to blame others and their circumstances (selfishness) instead of taking responsibility and admitting their sinful condition. When God spoke to the prophet Zechariah in chapter 7:8, 9, 11 concerning the hearts of the people of Israel, He stated:

And the Word of the Lord came to Zechariah: This is what the Lord Almighty says: "Administer true justice; show mercy and compassion to one another." But they refused to pay attention; stubbornly they turned their backs and stopped their ears. They made their hearts as hard as flint and would not listen to the law or to the words the Lord Almighty had sent by his Spirit through the earlier prophets.

History indicates that when God's people responded this way, what followed was the discipline of God. Discipline appeared to be punishment to the people of Israel, but it was done for correction for their good. The following verses speak to this issue:

My son, do not regard lightly the discipline of the Lord, nor faint when you are reproved by him; for those whom the Lord loves He disciplines, and He scourges every son whom he receives. It is for discipline that you endure; God deals with you as with sons; for what son is there whom his father does not discipline? (Hebrews 12:5–7, NASB)

All Scripture is inspired by God and profitable for teaching, for reproof, for correction, for training in righteousness; so that the man of God may be adequate, equipped for every good work. (2 Timothy 3:16)

We must pay more careful attention, therefore, to what we have heard, so that we do not drift away. (Hebrews 2:1)

Today, if you hear his voice, do not harden your hearts. (Hebrews 3:7)

See to it, brothers, that none of you has a sinful, unbelieving heart that turns away from the living God. But encourage one another daily, as long as it is called Today, so that none of you may be hardened by sin's deceitfulness. (Hebrews 3:12, 13)

The intended outcome of discipline is to develop godly character that keeps one walking in the ways of the Lord. When a man rejects the counsel of the Lord, his heart becomes hardened, which affects his conscience. There seems to be a downward progression of hardening of heart in the conscience, as humans continue to resist in disobedience. For instance, Paul speaks of a clear (pure) conscience in 2 Timothy 1:3: *I thank my God, whom I serve, as my forefathers did, with a clear conscience, as night and day I constantly remember you in my prayers.* 1 Timothy 1:5 states: *The goal of this command is love, which comes from a pure heart and a good conscience and a sincere faith.*

1 Corinthians 8:12 (NASB) warns: *And so, by sinning against the brethren and wounding their conscience when it is weak, you sin against Christ.* Titus 1:15 describes a defiled conscience: *To the pure, all things are pure; but to those who are defiled and unbelieving, nothing is pure, but both their mind and their conscience are defiled.* The author of Hebrews 10:22 explains: *Let us draw near with a sincere heart in full assurance of faith, having our hearts sprinkled clean from an evil conscience and our bodies washed with pure water.* Lastly, the seared conscience is described in 1 Timothy 4:1, 2: *The Spirit clearly says that in later times some will abandon the faith and follow deceiving spirits and things taught by demons. Such teachings come through hypocritical liars, whose consciences have been seared as with a hot iron.*

As counselors work with counselees, they pray for discernment concerning the heart of the counselees. Only God knows the heart, but a counselor works with counselees in determining their motivation. Just as a parent seeks to understand the heart of a child to determine whether the child's behavior is disobedient or defiant, a counselor needs to determine the motives of a counselee to understand how to proceed.

A counselor should reserve church discipline as a last resort. All resources, alternatives, and options should be considered before a counselor/pastor concludes that a matter must be taken to the church for discipline.

Church Authority

A member of a local church became involved in a sinful habit that was clearly in violation of God's Word. His actions were blatant and became known to church members and to the community. The pastor approached him and confronted him about his situation. Because of the extent of his prior involvement in the church, his response took the pastor somewhat by surprise. He said that the pastor should not concern himself with it, nor should anyone else from the church. He indicated that he knew his actions were wrong and sinful but involving the church or any church leader would be out of the question. He felt that he did not need to go through such a process and that such a procedure would be of no value to him or to anyone else. The pastor reminded him that he was a brother in the Lord and a member of the church, and that as such, he was accountable to the body of Christ—yet he remained unresponsive. In effect, this brother caught in sin was saying, "By what authority do you presume to confront me?" His perspective was one that totally rejected the authority of the church in disciplinary matters.

Sadly, this brother's attitude is not atypical in the contemporary congregation. It seems that church members often find the concepts of submission, ecclesiastical authority, accountability, and Christian community to be foreign ideas. Those who bother to address these issues at all are apt to find that what these individuals believe in their own hearts is in direct opposition to these concepts.

Faced with the prevalence of this thinking, church leaders would be wise to reexamine the issue of church authority. In the church of Jesus Christ, are members to be accountable to church leadership? That is, is the church endowed with authority? Was it correct to approach an errant member of the congregation, or was he right in his belief that the pastor was imposing and interfering where he did not belong? Some ancillary questions are raised by the story of this erring brother. What about judging the actions and behavior of others? Does the church have the right to judge? If the church does judge, is it being unloving? A major assumption by many is that discipline by a church proves that its members are rigid, judgmental, uncaring, and unloving.

To begin to examine the question of church authority, let's examine a representative sampling of relevant Scripture. Foundational to the issue of authority is the character of the church itself and the nature of proper relationships between members. The following passage crystallizes the essence of the environment in which church authority is to be exercised. *If one member suffers, all suffer together; if one member is honored, every part rejoices with it* (1 Corinthians 12:26). This concise statement gives a clear picture of a body bound inextricably together. Many other passages describe the loving, caring commitment to one another which is supposed to characterize the church. Yet, along with instructions to encourage and sympathize with each other, believers are also to obey commands charging them with a variety of disciplinary responsibilities, as the following Scriptural passages indicate.

> *Brothers, if someone is caught in sin, you who are spiritual should restore him gently. But watch yourself, or you also may be tempted. Carry each other's burdens and in this way, you will fulfill the law of Christ.* (Galatians 6:1, 2)

> *If your brother sins against you, go and show him his fault, just between the two of you. If he listens to you, you have won your brother over. But if he will not listen, take one or two others along,*

so that every matter may be established by the testimony of two or three witnesses. If he refuses to listen to them, tell it to the church; and if he refuses to listen even to the church, treat him as you would a pagan or a tax collector. (Matthew 18:15–17)

These passages are only a very few samples of the many passages indicating the Scriptural authority, judicial, and administrative responsibilities of the church. Indeed, the exercise of such authority is not just recommended, it is clearly commanded.

Prevalent Attitudes by Church Leaders

The attitude of leaders toward this subject varies, ranging from desiring to do church discipline but feeling inadequate and untrained to do so, to desiring to have no part of it due to fear of a disastrous conclusion. Both attitudes are understandable, but not justified. In a day when litigation is common practice, the church cannot hide her head in the sand and claim ignorance. If the church is to be the church of Jesus Christ and be obedient to His commands, she must take church discipline seriously.

Many churches seem to respond one of two ways when addressing this matter. The first is a rigid, hardline approach that is legalistic in nature and uncaring in attitude. This approach leaves the wounded members to survive on their own. It conveys to the sinner a "shape up or ship out" mentality. The second is a passive approach, which wants to be so understanding in nature and loving in attitude that it becomes impotent and does nothing. This style does not want to rock the boat or make waves. To judge or attempt to correct a brother might be misconstrued as being unloving or uncaring; therefore, the fellowship degenerates into a compromising, unholy position.

Issues such as liability insurance, membership covenants, and seminars and training sessions on church discipline must all be considered. Churches must grapple with proper policies, church constitutions and bylaws, signed documents, and filing and screening procedures.

The role of counseling is crucial if a church is to be successful in restoring a brother into fellowship. Who should counsel? Church leaders? Church members? What training in counseling should be given? Is it appropriate to involve the church community in counseling and discipling? The challenge for the church today is not to be paralyzed with uncertainty or lack of assertiveness in discipline. Christ extends to the church His authority for her to function in His name. It is time for her to exercise such authority for her good in striving toward purity and holiness in her fellowship.

What Determines Church Discipline?

When addressing church discipline, church leaders and members of a church must agree on what requires discipline. Answers to this question seem to vary, depending on such situations as when members have unresolved personal differences, those who persist in sin with an unrepentant spirit, divisive members within the church, and teaching doctrine contrary to the doctrine of the church. Such a list misses the point. What triggers the need for church discipline is when the offender refuses to listen and will not repent.

Who Should Be Disciplined?

Sins are not listed in Matthew 18:15–17. Jesus speaks to the condition of a man's heart and his willingness to listen, which would lead to repentance and reconciliation. When this doesn't happen, the unrepentant attitude calls for church discipline. Members of the body of Christ should, out of concern, go to any offender to seek restoration and reconciliation. The church leadership also has the responsibility to seek reconciliation with the offending party. When people voluntarily associate themselves faithfully with a local fellowship, they are then to be accountable to that group, whether or not they are technically members.

Counseling and Church Discipline

It has been established that church discipline is to be done by church leaders and members of the local church. It has also been established that the church receives authority to discipline from the head of the church, Jesus Christ. This leads to a very important consideration having to do with the role of counseling within the framework of church discipline. The church needs to grapple with who should counsel. The Holy Spirit has a role in counseling, and the church community has a role in counseling. Unfortunately, the church has shied away from this important ministry. If it is done within the church, it is usually the pastor who does it. The church needs to develop a Christlike attitude of compassion, listening, and healing as her goal. The church needs the vision of being an extension of the incarnation through genuineness, warmth, and understanding. Such a climate within a fellowship will establish a foundation on which to develop effective counseling. It falls on the pastor and church leaders to strive for and create such a climate.

The Christian involved in counseling has the advantage that the Holy Spirit can assist in the counseling process. It is the work of the Holy Spirit to convict sin (John 16:7–11), to give new life (John 3), and to give insight and understanding (John 16:13; 1 Corinthians 2:9, 10). The counselor needs the help of the Holy Spirit for strength and guidance. Counseling means engaging in spiritual warfare with the evil one. When another believer is involved in sin or disputes with another, the spiritual battle can be intense, as the forces of evil clash in warfare against truth.

A counselor needs to be equipped for the spiritual battle (Ephesians 6:11–18), as well as filled (controlled) by and walking with the Spirit (Ephesians 5:18; Romans 8:5–11). The greatest need in counseling is to rely on the Holy Spirit as the change factor, for without His work, no human is fully changed. A counselor must allow the Spirit to oversee the counseling activity. Along with the work of the Holy Spirit, and the use of Scripture, a counselor must consider the place of prayer in counseling. A counselor should pray for solutions to problems and for guidance and help from the Lord.

The Role of Community

The community of believers must be a witness of a compassionate God before the world. The word "compassion" is derived from the Latin words "pati" and "cum," which together mean "to suffer with." This is stressed in 1 Corinthians 12:26: *if one part suffers, every part suffers with it; if one part is honored, every part rejoices with it.*

Before anyone goes to others and confronts them with their sinful conditions, the confronter must examine his or her heart. Is it a heart of compassion? Is the goal and motive right before God? To be successful, confrontation must come out of a caring community. I overheard some men sharing in church, and one man stated that he saw himself as a fruit inspector. Another man said to him, "I hope you don't bruise the fruit as you inspect!"

A loving, compassionate fellowship enables members to carry each other's burdens and share each other's joys as witnesses to the compassionate Lord. Confrontation therefore flows from a supportive fellowship seeking healing within that fellowship in the context of biblical confrontation. As previously stated, 1 Timothy 1:5 (NASB) gives the motive: *But the goal of our instruction is love from a pure heart and a good conscience and a sincere faith.*

The church desperately needs to be a redemptive community offering forgiveness to those who have yielded to sin. Scripture states that God compassionately and truly cares about what happens to us (Romans 12:1; 1 Corinthians 1:3), and we are called to imitate our heavenly Father (Luke 6:36) and let His kind of caring bind believers to each other in unity (Philippians 2:1; Colossians 3:12).

The ministry of the church is to act as an instrument for bringing people back to God and to others. It is to facilitate a process in which estranged relationships are restored and reunited. In church discipline, the goal is reconciliation. Reconciliation is a gift, a surprise, grace; it cannot be forced. All the church can do is create an environment for it to happen. In *Making Peace*, Van Yperen supports this position, writing, "The goal of God for discipline and restitution is always restoration. He desires that we be restored to Him. God allows conflict in order that we might see our darkness and seek out the light. He has called us into the church so that we might be confronted, corrected, and encouraged to change" (2002, p. 247).

Discipleship and Counseling

The church does an injustice to an erring individual when the steps of confrontation, repentance, and forgiveness are taken and then the process stops. An ongoing discipline program is needed to nurture believers and provide a supportive system wherein believers are accountable to one another. Restoration of an erring brother is more than warm fuzzies. It takes work, time, and resources to restore a repentant brother to active service. Such a program of discipleship must consider one-on-one discipling and the networking of resources within the fellowship.

Established programs on discipleship seek to nurture and bring the individual to full restoration and wholeness. Trained leaders in the church should be assigned to certain cases, with the pastor or head counselor monitoring their work. The goal in a discipling program is personal spiritual growth. Disciples must learn how to develop biblical patterns by actual practice in responding to life's problems. To do this, they must learn to do God's will, which they discover in Scripture.

The second part of such a program is networking the resources within the fellowship. An erring brother or sister often needs help in more than one area of life. Sin entangles an individual into a web of trouble and problems. The local church is the body of Christ, gifted and talented in many fields. The erring member probably needs not only spiritual help (discipling), but also practical help in decision making, marital counseling, child rearing, and the like. The body of Christ is equipped to address most issues faced by an erring individual.

If the pastor spends some time training, organizing, and monitoring such a program, his ministry would be extremely enhanced and the members serving as counselors of his church would be excited about being part of such a networking ministry.

Modeling Influence

A byproduct of such a system is proper Christian modeling. Generally, when people have to go through church discipline, they have had poor models in their lives. The Apostle Paul spoke to the believers at Thessalonica concerning the issue of being unruly or undisciplined. He exhorted the believers to stay away from such "unruly" brothers, because they lived disorderly lives, lives without order or arrangement. Paul then admonished them, saying: *You yourselves know how you ought to follow our example. We were not idle when we were with you, nor did we eat anyone's food without paying for it. … We did this not because we do not have the right to such help, but in order to make ourselves a model for you to follow* (2 Thessalonians 3:7, 9). Paul stresses the importance of modeling, or being a good example, in teaching how to structure living. Also, in Philippians 4:9 Paul used his own life as a model to consider: *Whatever you have learned or received or heard from me or seen in me—put it into practice. And the God of peace will be with you.*

Teaching and preaching are one thing, but living it is another. The old saying "more caught than taught" holds true in this case. Often principles can be permanently and vividly impressed upon others by means of example. Paul challenged the Philippian church in 3:17: *join with others in following my example, brothers, and take note of those who live according to the pattern we gave you.* As people in the church take heart to these words by Paul, problems can be solved through a network of resourceful members serving as models or patterns for others. Such living testimonies leave lasting impressions for both the young and the old in the church fellowship.

Guidelines for Discipline

As you apply the guidance in previous chapters of this book, you will be able to address church discipline. I assure you that no matter what system you use or how kind, gentle, and skilled you are in counseling, there is no guarantee as to the outcome. However, such a reminder should not cause the church to cower and ignore the command to exercise church discipline.

In one of her columns, a famous advice giver responded to a question asked by one of her readers. The question was: "What should you do when you find one of your fellow church members sinning?" She wrote, "Mind your own business," or "pretend you never found out." This answer typifies modern thinking, as well as the thinking of many in the church today.

The church's role in church discipline is founded upon the authority of Christ. A mandate has been given by Jesus Christ to His church to conduct herself before the world as a model exemplifying purity and righteousness until He returns. In his book *Making Peace* (2002), Van Yperen wrote that every church should have guidelines for confronting sin redemptively. The following steps come from chapter 11:

- Upon discovery of sin in your life or the life of a fellow believer, go promptly and lovingly confess or confront the fellow believer in private (Matthew 5:23; 18:15).

- If the fellow believer listens and renounces sin, grant forgiveness in Jesus' name (Matthew 18:15, 21–35).

- If the sinner refuses to listen, return to admonish the believer again in the presence of one or two witnesses (Matthew 18:16).

- If the sinner still refuses to listen, the matter should be brought before your church leaders (Matthew 18:17). The leaders should investigate the matter carefully and thoroughly, discussing the specific charges with the believer.

- If there is no evidence of repentance, or if the believer refuses to cooperate in the process, the church body should be made aware of sin (Matthew 18:17).

- If there is still no evidence of repentance, fellowship with this believer should be broken until there is repentance (2 Thessalonians 3:6, 14; 1 Corinthians 5:11; Titus 3:10–11).

- God gives the church authority to "bind" and "loose," to withhold fellowship and to forgive (Matthew 18:18).

My humble attempt throughout this book has been to be biblical, practical, and realistic. I've stressed the need for training, modeling, discipling, and using knowledge of the Word of God as one's final and superior authority in all matters related to counseling. The significance of networking God's people is to assist the church leadership in counseling to exemplify godly wisdom and Christlike character in the context of Christian compassion and love for God and others.

Church Lifestyle Statement

We try to keep rules to a minimum, but obviously there must be some guidelines for any number of people to live and work together in an orderly way. The ideal is the Christian who concluded that he could do anything he pleased because the thing he pleased to do most was to glorify God in all his actions. This is our ideal, and we expect our members to accept the responsibility for voluntary self-discipline in striving to achieve it.

This presupposes an initial commitment to the Lord Jesus Christ as Savior by those who accept membership in our church. It is true that members may come from various backgrounds and from all stages of Christian maturity. It is our desire that each member will develop a Christian (biblical) worldview toward life. That all members will relate to the Lord Jesus all their knowledge, appreciations, skills, and motivations, and that they will learn to apply those attributes meaningfully to the purposes of Christ in the world. The emphasis here is not upon withdrawal from society, but upon the mission to society. All vocations are viewed as callings by the committed Christian.

Our concern is the development of a lifestyle appropriate to Christians in the twenty-first century. We believe that a qualitative difference should exist between the Christian and the unbeliever. Equally devout Christians hold different points of view regarding the conduct of the believer, and we recognize that divergent opinions will always exist. Nevertheless, we accept certain principles that constitute our approach to Christian distinctiveness in social practices, and we emphasize these to our members. Among these are the following:

- A wholesome philosophy of Christian conduct can best be developed in an atmosphere of personal freedom.

- Most issues are not black and white, and each Christian must learn to make thoughtful discriminations.

- Conduct not dealt with specifically in the Scriptures must be guided by the general principles to be found in the Bible.

- A Christian sense of values should lead to both appreciation and criticism of our culture.

- Christians might well establish their conduct on the conservative side of social practices.

- Dynamic spiritual power is directly related to voluntary personal discipline.

- The personal rights of the Christian must be subordinate to the corporate good of our fellowship.

- Compulsory obedience to a set of rules can never take the place of voluntary abandonment to the Lord Jesus Christ.

These are general principles by which our behavior is to be guided. Hopefully, legalism and negativism are avoided as much as possible to place primary stress upon a personal, vital relationship to Jesus Christ as Lord. At the same time, certain cautions have been highlighted in such universal biblical principles as refraining from practices that may tend to become addictive: *Everything is permissible for me — but not everything is beneficial. Everything is permissible for me — but I will not be mastered by anything* (1 Corinthians 6:12).

Because certain social practices are detrimental to the common good of our fellowship, it is expected that members will order their behavior in the light of these guidelines in all places and under all circumstances. Before seeking membership with us, we ask you to determine whether you can live comfortably within this kind of social structure. It is not our desire to exclude anyone from joining our membership who has first made a commitment of their life to Jesus Christ as their Savior. However, if you would find it difficult to live your life by the guidelines mentioned previously, we can only encourage you to worship with us regularly, and to search the Scriptures with us to determine the value of such a set of guidelines for you personally. Our hope is that the Lord will lead to us those who have already chosen this kind of Christian lifestyle for themselves and who in the process of expressing it will find their highest self-fulfillment in honoring and glorifying the Lord Jesus Christ.

Closing Thoughts

14

Does Biblical Counseling Work?

I've had the privilege of teaching biblical counseling on a college and seminary level. Many students have graduated and are serving as counselors in local churches and give witness to God's work of changing lives through various counseling programs. A sample listing of counseling programs comes from the work of one of those students, who served as the director of biblical counseling at her church.

Grief share—for individuals grieving the loss of a loved one (video, workbook, and discussion).

Divorce care—for individuals navigating an unwanted transition from marriage to single life (video, workbook, and discussion).

Crossroads (Ed Welch)—for addiction, specifically to drugs and alcohol.

Financial Peace University (Dave Ramsey)—for individuals wanting to work on finances.

Victory over Sexual Abuse—for women wanting healing from past abusive experiences.

By adding groups to the ministry, we were able to have biblically trained leaders reaching and serving more people in a congregation that has grown to 5,000. We are humbled and grateful to have watched this ministry grow as it served thousands of hurting people, bringing them biblical help, encouragement, and hope.

A Personal Testimony

The following testimony explains a personal involvement I had with a man dealing with alcohol, court intervention, and the exposure of a skeptical social service counselor to biblical counseling.

During the time I was teaching and counseling at the Biblical Counseling and Educational Center at Calvary Bible College and Theological Seminary, I received a phone call asking me to meet with an individual who had been arrested for driving under the influence of alcohol. This individual indicated that he was a Christian and communicated at his court appearance that he wanted to get Christian counseling. Under state law, the court system must grant such an individual religious counseling along with the legally mandated social services counseling intervention. The individual informed me that following his counseling by both parties, he was to return to court to appear before the judge. The social service department (the counselor assigned by the court) would present to the judge a report regarding the individual and an assessment by the counselor regarding the client's progress, which shall determine the sentence given by the judge.

I began meeting with the counselee once a week and I requested that his wife attend with him to hear my counsel and give any input regarding his addiction and addictive behavior. I did not want her to be in the dark as to what was being said in the counseling sessions. People struggling with addictions unfortunately have a way of twisting what was communicated or what occurred at a counseling session, using excuses, lying, and denial. Although they may appear very sincere and persuasive, they often also lie to the counselor if someone isn't there to verify the counselee's responses.

Shortly after meeting with John (not his actual name), the social service counselor assigned to him called me. She understood that the court by law had consented to John's request to get Christian counseling. She was very skeptical of "Christian counseling" and wanted me to explain to her what my counseling approach was with those addicted to alcohol, and what training and educational background I had to enable me to counsel people with such problems.

I told her that I understood her concern and was pleased to share my philosophy and methodology of biblical (Christian) counseling, along with my experience, training, and educational background. I began with my educational background. She was quite interested when I told her I had received a master's degree and a PhD in biblical counseling. I informed her that I had served as a pastor for twenty-five years and during that time had served as a chaplain for a fire department, police department, prison, community college, and vocational-technical school. I explained that I was certified with two biblical counseling agencies and presently was the director of the Biblical Counseling and Educational Center, as well as counselor and chair of the counseling department at the seminary. She found my background fascinating but inquired as to what specific credentials I had to counsel those with addictions. I informed her that I did not have a specialized credential in addictions, but that my training had included seminars and other trainings in counseling the addicted. I sensed that she had an issue with this but nonetheless wanted to know my philosophy of counseling.

I explained to her that John had established behavioral patterns that had been influenced by his wrong thinking and attitude, which had become a way of life for him. These patterns were destructive to himself, his marriage, his family, and his workplace, and were potentially harmful to others when he was behind the wheel of a car. I continued to explain that I would work with him in identifying his motivation(s) as to why he drinks and to start a process of changing his thinking, attitude, and behavior. During the counseling procedure his wife would accompany him to listen to what was communicated in the sessions. I told the social worker that the Bible speaks directly about drunkenness and that John and I would examine what the Bible says from a biblical perspective. I went on to explain that the Bible speaks about the consequences of an addiction to alcohol. The two passages of Scripture are from Isaiah 28:7–8: *And these also stagger from wine and reel from beer: Priests and prophets stagger from beer and are befuddled with wine; they reel from beer, they stagger when seeing visions, they stumble when rendering decisions.* The second passage is found in Proverbs 23:29–35:

> *Who has woe? Who has sorrow? Who has strife? Who has complaints? Who has needless bruises? Who has bloodshot eyes? Those who linger over wine, who go to sample bowls of mixed wine. Do not gaze at wine when it is red, when it sparkles in the cup, when it goes down smoothly! In the end it bites like a snake and poisons like a viper. Your eyes will see strange sights and your mind imagine confusing things. You will be like one sleeping on the high seas, lying on top of the rigging. They hit me, you will say, but I'm not hurt! They beat me, but I don't feel it! When will I wake up so I can find another drink?*

I pointed out to her that this was written by the wisest man of his times and his description of an addict is timeless and relevant for today. She seemed to agree.

I communicated to her that a distinctive part of the counseling method that I practice is the growth projects that John would be assigned on a weekly basis. Growth projects include studying, reading, meeting with others, and restructuring his life patterns away from his old destructive patterns. This addresses his issues related to the way he thinks, which is out of line with biblical truth, as well as his attitude that impacts his behavior (actions). This process also holds him accountable and keeps him engaged in making the changes needed for his good. Growth projects also enable the counselor to gauge the counselee's progress or lack thereof. This system will reveal the proper steps needed to make the right changes in his life.

The social services person acknowledged to me that she had never heard of this approach or the use of growth projects, yet she seemed very interested to hear more.

I shared that if John was to be victorious over his addiction, he would need a healthy support system. I informed her that his wife would be counseled as to how not to enable him in his drinking habit, but instead find ways to encourage and support him. He would receive the assistance of his church by my recruiting a few men who had had the same issues with alcohol but were no longer struggling, having found victory over their addiction to alcohol. I told her that I considered meetings with others who were presently dealing with addictions to be counterproductive and of little value for John. However, meeting with those who had recovered could offer encouragement as examples and models of those who have "been there" but overcame their addiction. These men would make a commitment to meet with John once a week to encourage, support, and pray with and for him, and share their stories about how they recovered from their addiction. My point to her was that Christians are part of a community, a family, where we care for one another and desire that all members receive help no matter what their issues might be. An addict has learned to live with his addiction in secret, hoping that no one notices the severity of his problem. He usually doesn't seek help from others and is convinced that he can conquer it on his own. He lives in denial and doesn't feel or acknowledge that he really has a drinking problem. At this point the court-ordered counselor was tracking with me and kept agreeing with what I was saying.

I explained that as his counselor I would monitor his weekly progress. I would evaluate the five influences that God has provided for a life of success (prayer, Spirit of God, Word of

God, family of God, and the church of God) and maximize these influences for a quicker recovery. John must recognize that he has personal responsibility—"skin in the game"—if he is to make progress. I also expressed to her that John had a great challenge in his life. I said that I did not have a magic wand to heal John from his addiction, but he had a great God and support system that believes in him and desires him to recover and not to be defeated but to have victory!

I told her the story about Jesus, who approached an invalid at the side of the Bethesda pool and asked the man an intriguing question: *Do you want to get well?* The man's condition had been that way for thirty-eight years! What kind of question is that? I believe it is a very profound question which repeated time and time is again, generation after generation, by people stuck in their addiction without knowing a way out. The question for John is crucial: *Do you want to get well?* The invalid responded to Jesus by saying, *I have no one to help me.* The story continues with Jesus healing the man: Scripture states that *at once the man was cured* (John 5:1–9). John must be honest with himself and realize he has a need; he must face it head on, seek the help of God for his life, and utilize the support system from other Christians. I explained to her that the pool of Bethesda means "home of incurables," a place of pain and sorrow, wretchedness and despair. John was also dealing with the sin of stubbornness, rebellion, anger, fear, and worry. The biblical counseling process changes such patterns by the process of eliminating negative traits and replacing them with correct virtues. I acknowledged that this might take a while, and that it was up to John. Would he be willing to do the hard work of implementing the process that moves him forward with positive change?

I said to this lady that as a biblical counselor, I must confront John directly about his condition. John is at the crossroads of life and he needs more than a once-a-week counselor; he needs a plan that includes everyone around him—his wife, family, church, counselors—all to encourage, support, and hold him accountable. He will face the highs and lows of his battle with alcoholism. I must challenge John regarding his motivation, his thinking, his attitude, and his behavior. He will at times lie, be deceptive, make promises yet quickly break them. He will be manipulative, shifting blame for his problems upon his circumstances and others, and seeking to foist guilt on those who are trying to help him. The bottom line is that John seeks control, yet in the process is losing all control. John must realize the power of sin and the bondage it creates for his life. As for all addicts, the consequences become apathy, hopelessness, and helplessness. As the saying goes, "the prisoner comes to love his chains." He needs forgiveness, healing, and a new life through Jesus Christ. I read to her Romans 4:7–8: *Blessed are they whose transgressions are forgiven, whose sins are covered. Blessed is the man whose sin the Lord will never count against him.* John has lived with self-defeatism, shame, and powerlessness for a long time. It's time for him to be restored.

I raised questions about the common belief that alcoholism is a disease. That is not to say alcoholism can't lead to a deleterious physiological condition, such as liver disease, heart trouble, brain damage, and other biological complications due to excessive drinking of alcohol over time. Nevertheless, to conclude that his addiction to alcohol is a disease is contrary to medical science. His drinking is a choice that has led to his addiction. The author of Lost Connections, Johann Hari, made an excellent point: "Your genes can certainly make you more vulnerable, but they don't write your destiny" (2018, p.148).

After this lengthy phone conversation with the social worker, I'll never forget her response. "That is a fascinating approach. I have never heard of anything like it. I must say, when I called you I did not have much confidence in 'Christian counseling.' I assumed you would tell me that you would meet with him a time or two, give him a few Bible verses with a pat on the back and tell him just to pray about your problem and all will be fine. I will add to my report for the court my confidence in the counseling technique you will be using with John."

I thanked her for her positive response and added one more thing. "Since we will both be counseling John, would you ask John in your sessions what he is learning from his Christian counselor? Ask him to show you the growth projects, materials he's receiving from me and have him verbalize what he's learning from me." I truly wanted to minister to her in an indirect way, for her to read and hear how biblical counseling was helping John. Not only did she agree to do that, she also surprised me with a question: "If I have other court cases in which they ask for Christian counseling, may I refer them to you?" Wow, I didn't see that coming, but I praise God for her confidence in giving me referrals.

John jumped through all the hoops of following the counseling schedule with both the social worker and me. To my knowledge, he has never been back in court for DWI. He is doing well and has a strong relationship with his family and church family.

The grace of God through Jesus Christ is our hope! Upon realizing what Christ has done for us, how should we then live? I believe the answer is to live out the life that has been set free from the shackles of sin. *Therefore, since we are surrounded by such a great cloud of witnesses, let us throw off everything that hinders and the sin that so easily entangles, and let us run with perseverance that race marked out for all of us. Let us fix our eyes on Jesus the author and finisher of our faith* (Hebrews 12:1–2). The outcome of such a life, in which sin is forgiven and guilt is replaced by gratitude and thanksgiving for all that Christ has done on our behalf, is truly a life liberated! *And whatever you do in word, or deed, do all in the name of the Lord Jesus, giving thanks through Him to God the Father* (Colossians 3:17).

This book has been an argument to support the title of this last chapter: Does biblical counseling work? I hope that it may serve as a guide, a "how-to" manual for the local church that desires to have an effective biblical counseling ministry. The reader will determine if the argument is convincing and, more importantly, if it will be useful for the church. I believe with all my heart that this is God's way, and it works! I rest my case.

Appendix A

Biblical Counseling Definition

Jay Adams. "For counseling to be biblical, it must be Bible-based, Christ-centered, and local church-oriented. Nouthetic counseling accepts the premise that the Bible is God's Word (II Tim. 3:16–17) and that it is totally sufficient for meeting all our needs (II Peter 1:3–4). Nouthetic counseling embraces three ideas from the Greek word *nouthesis* which are confrontation, concern, and change. To put it simply, nouthetic counseling consists of lovingly confronting people out of deep concern in order to help them make those changes that God requires."—Jay Adams, pastor, author, and founder of the biblical counseling movement and founder of the Institute for Nouthetic Counseling. Author of *Competent to Counsel.*

Henry Brandt. "Biblical counseling will be referred to as any person (pastor, teacher, husband, wife, friend, etc.) who uses the Word of God as the foundation for sharing truth with a person who needs to 'escape the corruption in the world caused by evil desires' (II Peter 1:4)."—The late Henry Brandt, former author and marriage and family counselor.

James Clark. "Biblical counseling is primarily in the context of the local church where a mature believer having knowledge of the Word of God comes alongside of another believer with a compassionate and empathetic heart to assist and guide that believer in the way of righteousness. This counseling process is to align the thinking, attitude, and behavior of an individual in accordance to the will of God as communicated in the Scriptures. This counseling approach seeks to be solution driven according to a biblical worldview. Elements of biblical counseling consider the work of the Holy Spirit, the exercise of prayer, and the encouragement of the members of the body of Christ. The outcome is to glorify God as it relates to the physical, mental, emotional, social and spiritual aspects of life." *Whether you eat or drink or whatever you do, do it all for the glory of God* (1 Corinthians 10:31).—Dr. James Clark, President Emeritus and former chair of the biblical counseling program at Calvary University, Kansas City, Missouri.

Joshua Clutterham. "Biblical Counseling is the whole counsel of God delivered in a systematic, understandable, relevant, and loving manner."—Joshua Clutterham, academic dean and chair of the biblical counseling program at Brookes Bible College, St. Louis, Missouri.

Faith Ministries. "Biblical counseling is the process where the Bible, God's word, is related individually to a person or persons who are struggling under the weight of personal sin and/or the difficulties with suffering, so that he or she might genuinely change in the inner person to be pleasing to God."—Faith Ministries, Lafayette, Indiana.

Ian Jones. "We acknowledge the revealed truth of God in the Bible and accept Scripture as the infallible standard by which all values, ideas, and concepts are evaluated. The Bible, through the illumination of the Holy Spirit, gives us the true and undistorted picture of human nature, our purpose, and how we are related to our creator. It is the standard by which we are able to interpret and make sense of the general revelation of God in creation."—Ian Jones, chair of the Division of Psychology and Counseling at Southwestern Baptist Theological Seminary, Fort Worth, Texas.

Luther Smith. "Biblical Counseling truly seeks to address not just moral change, or a behavioral adjustment. A biblical counselor seeks to address an individual's faulty worldview. A biblical counselor uses God's Word to confront a person's perspective that runs against Scripture and challenges the person to submit themselves to be transformed by God's Word."—Dr. Luther Smith, chair of the Biblical Counseling undergrad department, Calvary University, Kansas City, Missouri.

Paul Tautges. "Biblical counseling is an intensely focused and personal aspect of the discipleship process, whereby believers come alongside one another for three main purposes: first, to help the other person to consistently apply Scriptural theology to his or her life in order to experience victory over sin through obedience to Christ; second, by warning their spiritual friend, in love, of the consequences of sinful actions; and third, by leading that brother or sister to make consistent progress in the ongoing process of biblical change in order that he or she, too, may become a spiritually reproductive disciple-maker. Biblical counseling is helping one another, within the body of Christ, to grow to maturity in Him."—Paul Tautges, pastor, counselor, teaching fellow with the Association of Certified Biblical Counselors, and author.

Appendix B

Resources

Note: There are many other sources for training in the local church. This is simply an initial list for the church to consider.

Recommended books on theology:

Paul Enns. *The Moody Handbook of Theology.* Moody Press, 1989. A pastor may pick and choose chapters to discuss that would be pertinent for his team to develop a good theological foundation.

H. Wayne House. *Charts of Christian Theology and Doctrine.* Zondervan, 1992. A counselor would do well to understand the attributes of God, the names of God, anthropology, soteriology, and ecclesiology.

Charles Ryrie. *Basic Theology Survey.* Moody Press, 1986.

Recommended books on counseling for the local church:

Jay Adams. *How to Help People Change.* Zondervan, 1986.

Marshall and Mary Asher. *The Christian's Guide to Psychological Terms* (foreword by Wayne Mack). Focus Publishing, 2004.

John C. Broger. *Self-Confrontation: Biblical Counseling Foundation.* Capstone, 1991.

Ian Jones. *The Counsel of Heaven on Earth.* B&H Publishing, 2006.

John MacArthur & the Master's College faculty. *Counseling— How to Counsel Biblically.* Thomas Nelson, 2005.

Keith R. Miller. *Quick Scripture Reference for Counseling Men.* Baker Books, 2014.

Keith R. Miller & Patricia A. Miller. *Quick Scripture Reference for Counseling Youth* (updated and revised). Baker Books, 2014.

———. *Quick Scripture Reference for Counseling Couples.* Baker Books, 2017.

Patricia A. Miller. *Quick Scripture Reference for Counseling Women* (updated and revised). Baker Books, 2013.

George Sanchez. *Changing Your Thought Patterns.* Reprinted by Biblical Counseling Network (permission granted by the author). This booklet may be purchased by emailing bcnetwork@juno.com.

Paul Tautges. *Counsel One Another—A Theology of Personal Discipleship.* Day One Publications, 2009.

———. *Counseling One Another—A Theology of Interpersonal Discipleship.* Shepherd Press, 2015.

Milton Vincent. *A Gospel Primer.* This booklet may be purchased through Focus Publishing: www.focuspublishing.com.

Resources for changing lives:

Day One Publications. Booklets for living in a fallen world. Send email to sales@dayone.co.uk, or go to www.dayone.co.uk.

P&R Publishing, a Ministry of the Christian Counseling and Educational Foundation. https://www.prpbooks.com. Excellent topical booklets for reading, counseling, and making available at the church.

Recommended training sources:

The Annual Conference of Faith Church (Lafayette, Indiana): https://www.faithlafayette.org/biblical-counseling-training-conference

Center Biblical Counseling: https://biblicalcounselingcenter.org/resource-center

Regional training events:

Association of Certified Biblical Counselors (ACBC). 5401 N. Oak Trafficway, Kansas City, MO 64118.

International Association of Biblical Counselors. IABC Headquarters, P.O. Box 127, Broomfield, CO 80038; email: information@iabc.net. Member Services: P.O. Box 631, Mountain City, GA 30562; email: memberservices@iabc.net. URL: https://biblicalcounseling.com/training-2/acbc-regional-events/.

Local programs developed by ACBC Training Centers:

https://biblicalcounseling.com/training-centers/

Appendix C

Growth Project

(To be used before each session)

Counseling Checklist. Please take a moment before your counseling session to answer these questions.

1. This week I sincerely prayed about my problems, asking God to assist me in seeking His solutions to my circumstances. _____ Yes _____ No

2. I attended church this past week with the intent of hearing God's Word as it applied to me. _____ Yes _____ No

3. I spent quality time in God's Word and prayed on a daily basis this past week. _____ Yes _____ No

4. I applied myself to the counseling assignments this past week believing God could use them to bring change in both my attitude and my behavior. _____ Yes _____ No

5. I took ownership of my sins that contribute to my present problem(s) by confessing them, putting them off, and replacing them with godly responses. _____ Yes _____ No

6. I continue to struggle in the area of (briefly state) _____
_____
_____

7. I am committed to the counseling process, looking to God for strength and help to overcome my problems.
_____ Yes _____ No

8. Even if change is painful, I'm determined to be honest and to take ownership as to my contribution to the problem, whatever the cost.
_____ Yes _____ No

9. My goal is to seek biblical change that will bring about a Christ-like character in me and that will bring glory to God.
_____ Yes _____ No

10. I realize that for growth to take place I must move toward the problem(s), not ignore, withdraw from, or deny them.
_____ Yes _____ No

If you had to mark a "no" on any of the questions, briefly note which one(s) and state why.

#_____. Explanation

_____

Appendix D

Application for Counseling

CONFIDENTIAL

This application is to be completed by all applicants involved in the counseling ministry of [name of the organization].

PERSONAL

Date _____

Name _____

Present Address _____

_____

Phone: Home (_____) _____

Cell (_____)_____

1.   Have you ever been convicted of child abuse or a crime involving actual or attempted sexual molestation of a minor? Yes _____ No _____

If yes, please explain (attach separate page, if necessary)

2.   Were you a victim of abuse or molestation while a minor? Yes _____ No _____

If you prefer, you may discuss your answer to this question with the director/supervisor rather than answering it on the form.

3.   Do you have a current driver's license?
Yes _____ No _____

License # _____

4.   Have you ever been convicted of a traffic offense?
Yes _____ No _____

If yes, please describe all convictions for the past five years.

CHURCH ACTIVITY

Are you a member of a church? Yes _____ No _____

Name, address, and telephone number of the church:

_____

_____

_____

_____

List the name(s) and address(es) of other churches you have attended regularly during the past five years: (list on separate paper)

PERSONAL REFERENCES

Name _____

Phone (____) _____

Address _____

_____

Name _____

Phone (____) _____

Address _____

_____

APPLICANT'S STATEMENT:

The information I have given in this application is correct and complete to the best of my knowledge. I agree that false information or significant omissions may disqualify me from further consideration for service and may be considered justification for dismissal if discovered at a later date.

I authorize any references or churches listed in this application to give you any information (including opinions) that they may have regarding my character and fitness for counseling. I release all such references from any liability for furnishing such evaluations to you, provided they do so in good faith and without malice. I waive any right that I may have to inspect references provided on my behalf.

Should my application be accepted, I agree to be bound by the guidelines and policies and to refrain from unscriptural conduct in the performance of my services on behalf of [name of organization].

Applicant's signature _____

Date _____

Witness: _____

Date _____

APPENDIX E

Limits of Confidentiality

All information disclosed within the session is confidential and may not be revealed without your written permission except for the purpose of supervision.

However, disclosure is *required by law* under the following circumstances: when a client intends to take harmful, dangerous, or criminal action against themselves or another individual; when a client or their family is likely to suffer threats, or the results, of harmful behavior; or where there is a reasonable suspicion of the abuse of elderly persons or children under the age of eighteen.

I have read and accept the terms of my limits of confidentiality.

NAME (please print) _____

SIGNATURE: _____

DATE: _____

Appendix F

Consent Release

PERMISSION SLIP

Permission to consult with _____

as deemed helpful by the counselor:

_____ Yes _____ No

_____

Signature

_____

Date

APPENDIX G

Consent of Minor

_____
(Date)

This is to certify that I, _____
                                    (Parent/Guardian)

have given consent for _____
                              (Minor Client)

to receive individual and/or family counseling from the [insert
name of church or organization]

_____
Minor Client Signature

_____
Parent/Guardian Signature

_____
Counselor

Bibliography

Includes suggested reading and in-text references

Adams, Jay E. *Competent to Counsel*. Grand Rapids, MI: Zondervan, 1970.

———. *The Christian Counselor's Manual*. Grand Rapids, MI: Zondervan, 1973.

———. *How to Help People Change*. Grand Rapids, MI: Zondervan, 1986.

Asher, Marshall & Mary. *The Christian's Guide to Psychological Terms*. Bemidji, MN: Focus, 2004.

Brandt, Henry. *Breaking Free — From the Bondage of Sin*. Eugene, OR: Harvest House, 1994.

Brandt, Henry, and Kerry Skinner. *The Word for the Wise: Making Scripture the Heart of Your Counseling Ministry*. Nashville, TN: Broadman & Holman, 1995.

Broger, John C. *Self-Confrontation: Biblical Counseling Foundation*. Capstone, 1991.

Brotherhood Mutual Insurance Company. *The Deacon's Bench*. Ft. Wayne, IN: BMIC, Summer 1995.

Bullis, Ronald K., & Mazur, Cynthia S. *Legal Issues and Religious Counseling*. Louisville, KY: Westminster/John Knox Press, 1993.

Chafer, Lewis Sperry. *Systematic Theology, vol. I*. Dallas, TX: Dallas Seminary Press, 1947.

Denney, Jon G. *Introducing the Doctrine of the Sufficiency of Scripture*. Los Angeles, CA: The Master's Seminary, 2018 [doctoral dissertation, D. Min.].

Eerdman's *Handbook to the History of Christianity*. Grand Rapids, MI: Wm. B. Eerdman's Publishing, 1977.

Elliot, A. Matthew. *Faithful Feelings*. Grand Rapids, MI: Kregel, 2006.

Enns, Paul P. T*he Moody Handbook of Theology*. Chicago: Moody Press, 1989.

Eyrich, Howard A. *Three to Get Ready*. Grand Rapids, MI: Baker Book House, 1991.

Forsyth, P. T. (n.d.). https://www.quotes.net/quote/13094.

Gangel, Kenneth O. *Biblical Leadership*. Wheaton, IL: Evangelical Training Association, 2006.

Glasser, William. *Reality Therapy*. New York: Harper & Row, 1965.

Hall, Macie. "Perry's Scheme—Understanding the Intellectual Development of College-Age Students." *The Innovative Instructor* blog. December 13, 2013 [blog post]. https://ii.library.jhu.edu/2013/12/13/perrys-scheme-understanding-the-intellectual-development-of-college-age-students/

Hari, Johann. *Lost Connections*. New York: Bloomsbury, 2018.

Hendriksen, William. *New Testament Commentary, I and II Thessalonians*. Grand Rapids, MI: Baker Book House, 1987.

Hessel, Victor E. *Phenomenological Study of Pastor Burnout*. Dissertation for Doctor of Management in Organizational Leadership degree, Phoenix University, 2014.

Hill, Gary. *Sword Discovery Bible New Testament*. La Habra, CA: The Lockman Foundation, 1987.

House, H. Wayne. *Charts of Christian Theology and Doctrine*. Grand Rapids, MI: Zondervan, 1992.

Jacobs, John. *Power Sword Discovery Bible New Testament with God's Power Promises*. Dallas, TX: World Bible Publishers, Inc, 1987.

Johnson, Eric L., & Stanton, Jones L. *Psychology & Christianity*. Downers Grove, IL: InterVarsity Press, 2000.

Jones, Ian F. *The Counsel of Heaven on Earth*. Nashville, TN: B&H Publishing Group, 2006.

Kilpatrick, William Kirk. *Psychological Seduction*. Nashville, TN: Thomas Nelson, 1983.

Kurtz, Paul, & Wilson, Edwin H. "Humanist Manifesto II" American Humanist Association, 1983. https://americanhumanist.org.

LaHaye, Tim. *Spirit-Controlled Temperament*. Wheaton, IL: Tyndale House, 1967.

———. *Transformed Temperaments*. Wheaton, IL: Tyndale House, 1971.

Levicoff, Steve. *Christian Counseling and the Law*. Chicago: Moody Bible Institute, 1991.

MacArthur, John. *Counseling: How to Counsel Biblically*. Nashville, TN: Thomas Nelson, 2005.

Maliska, Lee. *Foundations for a Multi-Church Sponsored Biblical Pastoral Care and Counseling Center* (PhD dissertation). Westminster Theological Seminary, 1988.

Mangalwadi, Vishal. *The Book that Made Your World*. Nashville, TN: Thomas Nelson, 2011.

Meier, Paul D., Minirth, Frank B., & Wichern, Frank B. *Introduction to Psychology and Counseling*. Grand Rapids, MI: Baker Book House, 1982.

Miller, Keith R. *Quick Scripture Reference for Counseling Men*. Baker Books, 2014.

———. *Quick Scripture Reference for Counseling Couples*. Baker Books, 2017.

Miller, Keith R. & Patricia A. *Quick Scripture Reference for Counseling Youth* (updated and revised). Baker Books, 2014.

Miller, Patricia A. *Quick Scripture Reference for Counseling Women* (updated and revised). Baker Books, 2013.

Montgomery, Dan & Kate. *Compass Psychotheology*. Albuquerque, NM: Compass Works, 2006.

Mueller, George. *Answer to Prayer from George Mueller's Narratives*. Chicago: Moody Press, 1984.

Pearcey, Nancy R. *Total Truth*. Wheaton, IL: Crossway Books, 2004.

Perry, William. Forms of Ethical and Intellectual Development in the College Years. New York, NY: Holt, Rinehart & Winston, Inc. 1970.

Piper, John. *Brothers, We Are Not Professionals*. Nashville, TN: Broadman & Holman, 2002.

Richards, Lawrence O. *Expository Dictionary of Bible Words*. Grand Rapids, MI: Zondervan, 1985.

Ryrie, Charles. *Basic Theology Survey*. Moody Press, 1986.

Sanchez, George. *Changing Your Thought Patterns*. Reprinted by Biblical Counseling Network (permission granted by the author). This booklet may be purchased by emailing bcnetwork@juno.com.

Sande, Kenneth. *The Peacemaker*. Grand Rapids, MI: Baker Book House, 2004.

Smith, Robert D. *The Christian Counselor's Medical Desk Reference*. Stanley, GA: Timeless Texts, 2000.

Tautges, Paul. *Counsel One Another—A Theology of Personal Discipleship*. Day One Publications, 2009.

———. *Counseling One Another*. Wapwallopen, PA: Shepherd Press, 2015.

Tripp, Paul David. *Instruments in the Redeemer's Hands*. Phillipsburg, NJ: P&R Publishing, 2002.

Van Yperen, Jim. *Making Peace*. Chicago: Moody Press, 2002.

Vincent, Marvin R. *Word Studies in the New Testament, Vol. III*. New York: Charles Scribner's Sons, 1924.

Vincent, Milton. *A Gospel Primer*. This booklet may be purchased through Focus Publishing: www.focuspublishing.com.

Vine, W. E. *An Expository Dictionary of New Testament Words*. Old Tappan, NJ: Fleming H. Revell, 1966.

Index of Scriptural Citations